Die

With a Smile

Spiritual Laws of Success

Mark Lore

D1738323

Die With a Smile: Spiritual Laws of Success

Copyright © 2024 Mark Lore

Contents

Foreword

When I was 35, I was a mess. My business was struggling, I was getting a divorce after a 13-year marriage, everyone hated me, and I was nearly financially bankrupt. I had to get loans to pay child support and alimony. My parents told me they were going to side with my ex-wife. My in-laws, whom I loved, wouldn't talk to me. And my kids were wounded and refused to tell me that they loved me. I had just opened my second store and was sleeping in the garage—alone—and completely depressed. But I had to perform each day for my employees, my children, and the banks and show that I was strong and together.

When I got divorced, I lost all of my friends. They were all married and didn't know how to interact with us now that we were splitting up. I called our three closest friends and told them to support my ex-wife because I knew that I would be okay once the dust settled, and she needed the support more than I did. I was sad and unhappy. Then someone—a longtime friend—handed me a book called <u>Many Lives, Many Masters</u> by Brian Weiss.

The book is about a doctor who happened to get people who had not responded to traditional psychotherapy into hypnosis and past life regressions. Someone once said that you don't find books, books find you, and never was that truer for me. I read that book in two nights and could not get enough of the mindset that there was much more to this conflicted, painful life than what I had learned thus far.

So, I began reading and listening to everything I could about the science of the afterlife and spirituality. There were amazing books about people who studied the energy changes in plants when humans interacted with them; books about quantum physics and how our thinking about something like a chair changes the molecular movement in that object; books about people who had near-death experiences, as well as people who have tapped into life between lives regression therapies.

My learning reminded me of the day my older brother told me that there was no Santa Claus or Easter Bunny. That day, all of the magic of life was sucked out of my little soul. Now, as I was learning, the magic of life was real and being rekindled again.

As I was learning that we are eternal and this current life is nothing more than an opportunity for our souls to evolve toward love, it opened up new avenues of awareness for me. I began to understand that I could either figure these lessons out and rest in peace and love in the spirit world or keep coming back and living lives that would teach me how to do this. Although I do love life, I much prefer not to be in a chaotic, violent, judgmental world and instead live in the wonderful world of the spirits where there is only love. My journey has opened my eyes to the fact that I only have two choices: either to evolve and open my mind to the new or not.

In my quest for the truth about this existence, I have learned that almost everything we believe and have been taught isn't true. This world and this life are a stage play with people and lessons brought into our lives to teach us the lessons of the spirit.

Over the three decades I have sought answers to the question of why we are here, I have learned many very powerful truths that I share in this book. Most people that I talk to about these ideas are blown away at the simplicity yet the powerful validity of these thoughts, which gave me confirmation that I was going down the right path.

Since I have learned and put these lessons into my life's daily practice, I am almost always happy and at peace. I never get sick. All of my relationships are satisfying and wonderful, even those that used to be adversarial. I have learned to live unconditionally, and it has made all the difference in terms of my chronic happiness.

I have read hundreds, maybe a thousand books, and virtually all of them were written by those who I considered more evolved than me. I always took notes and stuck them in a file labeled "The Book." When I finally decided that I was in a place where my education could help others, I pulled out that file and began writing. Throughout my years of note-taking, I had decided that if I read a book and got one great idea out of it, there was value in my endeavor. This book is a compilation of the best things I have learned. The problem I see, though, is that we are not taught much of this, and we have to figure it out on our own. For some people, it never happens in their lifetime because they don't know where or how to seek these truths. It's taken me three decades and I'm still learning, so this book is a summary of all that I've learned on my path of growth.

Max Planck, a German theoretical physicist credited with being the originator of quantum theory in the early 20th century, once said, "A new scientific truth does not triumph by convincing its opponents and making them see the light, but rather they eventually die and a new generation grows up that is familiar with it." That's a huge reason why we don't know more about the science of the afterlife. The people in power who write our curriculums, teach our children and adults, and lead our society as spiritual experts would have to admit they've been wrong for most of their lives.

Throughout my 60+ years of life studying and learning the human condition, I have primarily focused on the things we aren't taught as children. I have looked to provide answers as to why most people I know are only superficially happy, fraught with anxiety, depressed and sad, unfulfilled, in bad relationships, and usually unable to pull themselves out of this cycle of birth, pain, and death. Ever heard the saying, "Life sucks and then you die"? It's supposed to be funny, but deep down, anyone who hears it agrees with it at some level.

Through my constant seeking of the reasons for this common feeling among people, I believe I have uncovered the barriers to happiness and a fulfilled life. I've also learned that I don't have to work hard to be happy; I just have to identify and eliminate those barriers that keep me from being so. Getting there hasn't been easy, but it has been rewarding and illuminating, especially because as I have learned these truths, I was not discovering them but remembering them again since I know now that we are already wired with love and happiness as our natural state.

The immutable lessons I have learned examine the futility of our bodies and the inordinate importance we place on them. I know now that I hold all of the power to create the world around me that I want to see and be. I've largely shed my addictive conditioned responses to situations and other people. No longer will I waste my energy on my continuously erroneous judgments. There is a whole world of science now that proves we are connected with every living thing, and if we choose to understand our role in this world, we can start to know there is a collective consciousness. One of the ways this connection presents itself is through studies on remote viewing.

Stephan A. Schwartz has performed studies to determine if people can exhibit nonlocal consciousness and connect with people and places thousands of miles away. His experiments have come up with several key findings.

- Remote viewers have demonstrated an ability to accurately describe locations that they could not possibly see.
- Experiments have shown that remote viewers can identify objects located in different locations without any prior knowledge about them.
- Research has shown that remote viewing can be used to accurately predict future events.
- Results also indicate that sensory data obtained via remote viewing is often more accurate than sensing data obtained conventionally. This is how the United States military located Sadam Hussein.

Studies like those about remote viewing, Near Death Experiences (NDEs), and other areas of study not taught in our schools have shown me there is a whole world around us that I don't fully know yet. The world we think we see and know is nothing like we were taught. It's far more complex and intricate, yet simple and magical.

I hope you will get more than one life-changing idea out of this book. If you do, I have been successful. Gaining true knowledge isn't a light switch; it's more like a volume control knob that you learn to use with practice. I'm still practicing and would never go back now.

Chapter 1

The Soliloquy of Life

What do you believe happens when you die? Because you will die.

L et's say we don't die when we die. Let's say that we do remain in every sense ourselves, just without our current bodies. Our spirits were created as energy and we can't be "uncreated." Only our bodies are temporary, not our spiritual essence and personalities.

But why should you believe that? According to the evidence of everything we can see, touch, hear, and smell, death is indeed the end. Life stops, the body decays, and we're gone forever. Where's the evidence that the opposite is true? That the soul leaves the body, the body decays, and the soul continues in existence...forever. Even if you do believe in eternal life, you probably associate it with some organized religion. Maybe the one that says we're doomed to suffer on Earth, then doomed to suffer forever after, unless we're one of the chosen few.

Evidence of eternal life is so much less important than the real effects of simply believing that it's true. Once we believe it, so much in our lives changes for the better because we can start viewing this world through a different lens.

What is the world to us if our souls live on beyond the time we spend here? What can we let go of, and what do we choose to nurture, knowing that we are eternal?

Believing that we are eternal and live on beyond the body's death is so much more exciting and real than thinking we simply die and turn into dirt when this life ends. Plus, knowing that we are eternal gives more significance and meaning to this life. We are wired to fear death, yet that bridge between life and death is the wink of an eye. Accepting the truth of our eternal nature eliminates the nagging fear of death and brings a new wonderment to our transition to a different stage of eternal life.

Fuck turning into dirt! First of all, that's no fun, and secondly, there are mountains of evidence that it isn't at all true if one chooses to learn more about our actual lives on Earth and beyond from a spiritual perspective.

Thinking there is nothing after this life is fatalistic and simplistic. I don't think life is that simplistic. I think there's a reason we are here. I don't want to have to die to know how to live. So, I read every spiritual book I can get my hands on, and I decide the merit of the teachings based on how I feel. Feelings get a bad rap in our society because no one makes any money when you learn how to trust your feelings and follow their truth without the guidance of some "expert." But they're the best tool we have for connecting with our source of eternal truth.

That's why if some piece of so-called wisdom makes me feel at peace with myself, with others, and with whatever is going on in the moment, I believe it because it vibrates in tune with my eternal nature. If it makes me feel guilty, ashamed, afraid, oppressed, judgmental of myself and others, and generally not at peace -- into the fireplace it goes!

I had a pretty shitty childhood. No one is going to write a screenplay about it, but the nature of my upbringing, along with my human nature, set me up for a whole lot of misery. As far as my parents were concerned, I was a "dumb jock," an unrealistic idealist, chronically late, lazy, ungrateful little bastard -- and those were the compliments.

I was born in Oakland, CA. My father was severely wounded in the Korean conflict. When I was too young to remember, he would put a gun to my head when I cried, threatening to kill me if I didn't stop. Back then, PTSD was called "shell shock." He had it, and we had no cures.

My mother left him when I was young, and I lived in a duplex in Buffalo, NY, with my grandparents downstairs and my mother, my older brother, and me upstairs. She worked as an RN, so my grandma watched me. I got unconditional love from my grandparents until one day, when I was almost six, Peter showed up.

Peter was a corporate man. Unmarried. A good provider. He promised to make my mother a good husband. And to whip her two boys into shape.

I remember my first interaction with him. We moved from my grandparents' duplex to a house in Cheektowaga, NY. The first day we moved into that house, my brother ran out the back door, and as it was slamming shut, I put my arm out to stop it, and my arm broke through the screen. Peter saw it and proceeded to beat the shit out of me. I was six years old. I had never been hit before, and I remember thinking, "Who the fuck is this man?" Little did I know he was to be my tormentor for the next twelve years.

Not only did I get beaten regularly over those years, but Peter constantly told me what a loser I was. My mother always sided with him, so I quickly learned the game. At first, when he was hitting me, of course, I would cry. But by the time I was nine or ten, I had learned to show no emotion as he hit me.

That made me feel powerful because he couldn't hurt me beyond the short-lived physical pain.

Peter was such a little man, emotionally and spiritually. My parents were big people in the Catholic church and eager to show off their "perfect family." (They had three more kids of their own after they married). Once the "perfect family" got home from church, he would beat the snot out of me if I hadn't performed perfectly.

When I was sixteen, Peter slapped me across the face and I snapped. I picked him up and pinned him to the wall by his collar and told him if he ever touched me again, I would fucking kill him. He never did again -- although his insults never stopped.

But there's something to be said about childhood trauma. Many abused children aren't as lucky as I was, but for me, the main effect of the way my parents treated me was that I got angry. Really angry almost all the time. Even after I grew up and left home and tried to start down my path, I was pissed off and competed with everyone, whether they deserved it or not.

I once got so angry at my two-year-old son for throwing his dinner plate on the floor that I called him a "little fucker" and yelled so loud I made him cry, which only made me madder. The whole thing ended with me storming out of the house and drinking a fifth of whiskey on a park bench down the street before I went back home and tried to crawl into bed without waking up my wife.

In the morning, she wouldn't talk to me. I hardly wanted to talk to myself, but when I looked at my unshaven face in the mirror, I had one damn good question to ask. <u>Why the hell are you so angry, Mark?</u> I tried, but for the first time, I failed to convince myself that it was because of the green beans my son threw on the floor.

So, what was it? I got really curious about this. I tried on and threw out a grand bunch of theories.

I'm angry because my stepfather is an asshole.

Sure, makes sense that would make me angry in the past, but why now? Why today?

I'm angry because I could never be good enough for my mother.

Again, the past.

I'm angry because everyone is always trying to take advantage of me. I'm angry because I'm the only one who does any work around here. I'm angry because I married the wrong woman. I'm angry because it wasn't my idea to have a baby and the damn thing won't stop crying!

Around this point, I started to notice something. The more I considered what was making me angry, the more I realized I was angry because I was always justifying and rationalizing my behavior in my mind, and it was wrong. The anger, the competition, the battles with everyone were keeping me at war with the world. I had been taught that if I wanted to win the war of peace in this life, I had to win all the battles. I was starting to realize that, in fact, the only way to win the peace of my being was to stop fighting all of the battles. I knew this was true because it was so complete and final. War over. A peace treaty with myself and everyone I came in contact with.

I used to be petrified of death, especially my own, because I was in love with my ego -- and the ego does have an expiration date. One of the first truths I learned on my journey of seeking to understand this life is that we don't die; we simply change form. And this change of form is nothing but wonderful. It's a heck of a lot better than the crazy, chaotic life we may currently find ourselves in. But what I have learned in my search for the truth is that there is no chaos except what we individually cause. Most of the situations we put ourselves in, good or bad, are part of a master plan to bring us toward love.

I mentioned evidence earlier. Where is the evidence of eternal life? I was as surprised as you to find that there is a mountain of evidence from throughout the ages that shows us that when we die here on Earth, our spirits live on. What do you think the purpose of Jesus rising from the dead was? We weren't supposed to hang crucifixes all over the place because that memorialized Him being put to death. What we really should honor is the fact that He showed us that we don't die, not forever.

When I first started learning about our eternal nature, it gave me the profound sense of peace and freedom from anger I'd been seeking. So, I applied myself to reading many books and articles on the subjects of Near-Death experiences (NDEs), past-life regressions, Life Between Lives hypnotherapy (LBL), and other afterlife situations. Some people study these phenomena scientifically, while other stories seem embellished to sell more books. It's easy not to believe unless you learn it for yourself and stop accepting the dogma from people who haven't conscientiously studied the science behind it. Of course, most religious institutions ignore and conceal these facts, while our scientific elite calls it "junk science" because it goes beyond the small box they have put over their heads. I call it truth and it's the truth that breaks us free from the constraints of their limited societal rules.

The most compelling and well-documented studies, like those from Pim van Lommel, M.D., in his book *Consciousness Beyond Life,* have shown that people who have had Near-Death Experiences (NDEs) had at least five consistencies in their experiences while they were clinically dead. This shows that when we die, we don't get to choose what our outcome is, regardless of our beliefs. The consistencies are so similar and across a wide breadth of cultures, genders, ages, and times that I would have to be an idiot to ignore them and a fool to believe that I could create my outcome after death. There's no Hell where we burn and are tortured for our "sins." The concept of a vengeful judgment upon life's end is a man-made concoction to control our minds. It's powerful enough to limit our thinking and behavior, though, because it has been ingrained as "The way it is" for centuries.

The five experiences that are consistent with the thousands of people who have experienced NDEs are:

1. Everyone reports experiencing deep feelings of peace, surrender, bliss, and tranquility, all of which appear to be our most natural state -- that of pure love.

2. All reports go into an unearthly dimension of indescribable beauty with colors, sounds, and visions that are far more vivid and beautiful than even the greatest experiences on this earthly, physical plane.

3. Everyone speaks of going through a "life review," focusing on how they did or didn't love and forgive others but without judgment or condemnation.

4. In the death state, people describe how they could communicate with loved ones who had previously died and communicate without speaking.

5. The vast majority report that they were looking down on their dead body from a different vantage point and could see and understand everything that was happening to their bodies.

Some other consistent experiences from many people after they had their NDEs:

Fewer affiliations with religions and more spiritual connections, an enhanced intuitive sensitivity, enhanced synchronicity. (For example, thinking about someone just before they call.)

Afterward, people who experience NDEs are generally no longer afraid of death and take more pleasure in living a conflict-free life of peace and love. Materialistic things like status and making money no longer have the same importance.

When I learned these facts, I immediately became unafraid to fly. That had been a big fear of mine -- and I had to fly weekly for my job. I would get to the airport two hours prior to my flight and get hammered at the bar. One day, I was getting drunk at the bar, and I heard my name being paged over the airport speaker system. I was so late that the plane had waited a few minutes because of me. I was a mess. Only when I was no longer afraid of death did flying become fun again.

I also came to understand that my fear of death was proportionate to the pettiness and insignificance of my life. I began to understand that I am "in" this world today but not actually "of" this world.

Remember when you first found out that Santa Claus was bullshit? That was a cold day for me because not only had I just acquired a douchebag stepdad, but all of the magical "nice" fantasies I had believed went up in flames. When I learned about the reality of what happens upon death based on these studies, it was like finding out that Santa was real. Death is actually better than life! I don't want or expect to die anytime soon, but when I do (and I will), it's factually a very loving and peaceful place....and based on the evidence, I won't want to come back to this life.

Beyond NDEs, there are documented instances of people who have tapped into past lives, whether through hypnosis, comas, or other means, when the avenues of awareness beyond this world opened up to them. Speaking languages completely unknown to them, reciting facts that they could not possibly have known, and recalling past situations in other amazing and almost unbelievable ways are further evidence that we live on after this existence and have multiple lives. We can believe it or not, but it won't change the truth of our eventual outcome.

> There is a divine purpose to our lives today, and all the evidence points to our souls learning the lessons of love, forgiveness, and oneness.

That may seem like a fairy tale to some, especially when you are trying to pay the rent and someone is pissing you off, but now I simply consider those situations as an opportunity to react differently.

Let's say that you are a juror in a death penalty trial and the prosecution brings out a dozen credible witnesses who testify that they saw and experienced the events that prove the accused murdered the victim. All eye-witnesses for the crime, all with incredibly similar testimonies as to the events. Would you not vote to convict? (notwithstanding your views on the death penalty). The evidence laid out in the arguments about our eternal souls and multiple lives has far more credible witnesses than a dozen.

Once I had truly accepted that I was eternal and understood that there is a singular outcome upon death for all of us, I had to consider how it changed everything I had defined and judged in this life. There is so much more going on than we even know or are taught.

If we are eternal, how important are the little annoyances, conflicts, disagreements, judgments, and ego gratifications of this transitory life? They end when we die. We don't. My grandfather didn't talk to his brother for the final thirty years of their lives because one called the other a "cheater" at playing cards. Do you think anyone, including them, now that they are both dead, give a fuck about that card game? (Even though it was for money!) As for myself, I had harbored anger for years from people who had borrowed money without paying it back, insulted my ego, or simply pissed me off. For what? Was I going to carry that poison to my deathbed? Upon understanding that I was really eternal, I started giving up all that pointless anger toward others. Yes, even my shitty parents. No more of me drinking poison and hoping others got sick.

It was I who was freed.

Since I'm eternal and all the individual conflicts created or engaged in by me aren't, what real importance do any of these conflicts have? The friend who never paid me back, my parents' unfairness, my coworker who stole my idea, my spouse who cheated on me, or my ungrateful kids who won't eat their vegetables. None of that will matter one bit in twenty years, twenty minutes, or twenty seconds, so I'm learning to give up the anger immediately.

One thing that helped me deal with this newfound realization was to stop looking at my life as a series of individual events. I stopped looking at my life as individual good or bad actions that happen to me randomly and started trying to understand it from a 30,000-foot view. My life was a continuum of lessons and learning. By undergoing that change in perspective, all of these battles to win instead become lessons for me to learn. And all of the lessons seem to point me in the direction of learning to live without conflict. Next time, I won't lend money that I need to get back or care about what someone else said. I'm going to decide that all my other conflicts are over, and only I can keep carrying them on my back and alive in my mind.

Until we become convinced of our own immortality, we will continue to put misplaced focus on our bodies, our individuality, and our status in the world. This keeps us in the cycle of birth, pain, and death. Without understanding the true meaning of what we are doing in this life, we doom ourselves to conflict, death, and misery, whereas believing and knowing that we live on after this life gives new meaning to our existence.

But it doesn't happen all at once, without effort. It's not even permanent -- not as long as we still doubt our own immortality. For me, it took a lot of practice, giving up my judgments and my anger a little quicker each time until it became automatic. I remember the first time I recognized the feeling of rage in my body and then immediately watched it disappear. It didn't even linger for a second anymore!

The next time I went to visit my mom and stepdad at the nursing home, I put myself to the test. I listened to my stepdad try to guilt-trip me into calling more often because "all his friends' kids called more often," and it made him look bad. (Look bad, mind you -- not feel bad.) The familiar sensations of anger showed up, and I simply watched as they went on their way.

This time, watching the anger dissipate, I had a realization: My distressing feelings had nothing to do with me. They were temporary, so they could never belong to my real, eternal being. Now, at last, I really became free. Free to feel only the contentment and ease that come from being in harmony with my immortal soul -- and with all that is eternal in our universe. Free to love myself and others and to live my life on my terms. Free to see the truth and to share it with you.

> We are eternal and live on after this life. There is one outcome when we leave this world, and that is love. Whether we believe it or not is completely irrelevant.

Chapter 2

Many Lives, Many Lessons, One Outcome

A fter reading all of Brian Weiss' books, I sought out everything I could on past lives and the afterlife. I was so energized and excited to find out there was a much bigger plan for humanity than daily fighting for legal tender, status, and stuff. There are many books about reincarnation and the afterlife and a lot of them are actual case studies and real-world examples -- not merely myths and legends. There's a plethora of books that detail the Akashic Records, children who accurately talk about a past life with confirmed details they couldn't have possibly known, life between lives details corroborated by other unrelated individuals who have had near-death experiences or hypnotic regressions, and so much more proof of the afterlife. I looked for books that might debunk the idea of reincarnation and many lives and I found one book on that topic. It was unpersuasive to me as it delved mostly into the charlatans and fakes who have tried to make money pretending to talk to those who have passed. There was no scientific method that proved or supported the lack of a spiritual plane and an afterlife.

I did learn that 1500 years ago, the Roman Emperor, Justinian 1, removed all of the teachings of reincarnation from all Catholic doctrines, and in those days, if you questioned authority, you had a short life span, usually ending with your own funeral pyre. Within a couple of generations, no one questioned it anymore. Additionally, the Judeo-Catholic leaders of the day decided that reincarnation and rebirth went against their dogma and ideas that there was a strict reward and punishment for bad behavior in this one life. They wanted to promote a judgment from God that was eternal and complete. Religious "truths" have changed with the times, so how true can they be?

Most people today don't even consider that we live many lives because it's never talked about as a possibility when we are being schooled, yet I have learned that it is so true. Our "experts" and "holy" men say there's no proof of multiple lives because if they simply looked to see it, they would have to admit they have been teaching and believing lies for 1500 years.

> **If you don't seek the truth, it won't accidentally discover you.**

Hinduism and Buddhism believe in reincarnation and multiple lives. That means about 1.5 billion people -- people who are no different than you or I -- believe in reincarnation and continuous rebirth of our souls. I now know they are correct on that issue. Our religions have robbed us of the central truth of the reason we are here and what it means in our evolution. That's why many religious institutions are dying a slow death due to a lack of members. They give people partial truths as immutable, which makes the lies more difficult to expose.

What has convinced me over my decades of studying the afterlife was not gullibility. It was when I read or heard something so true that it left an indelible mark in my brain. The truth resonated with me and made me want to learn more. I have learned that I had a life before, now and next.

As I was writing this chapter, I went back to one of the books that transformed much of my thinking in a very positive way. *A Course in Miracles*, edited by Helen Schucman and William T. Thetford, delves into the idea of reincarnation, and I have found this book to clarify much of my thinking on various other life topics. To paraphrase *A Course in Miracles* – ultimately, reincarnation isn't possible in the strict sense of how we define it because there is no past or future. Time is a construct of this physical life because what is the meaning of time in eternity? A Course says, "To say that time is temporary is merely redundant. Time is a learning device that will be abolished when it is no longer useful."

What the Course says is that the concept of many lives is helpful so long as it is used properly. There are always positives to be taken from the thinking that the soul and the body are not the same and there are always dangers in arguing topics as controversial as reincarnation. Eliminating the individual ego is a task enough to cope with without bringing in a potentially incendiary topic such as that. All that must be known is that birth is not the beginning and death is not the end.

Typical of A Course *in Miracles* is that I had to read the passages dealing with reincarnation multiple times to fully understand what they were saying, and I'm still not sure I FULLY understand everything. Taken with my other learning, I have come to firmly believe that we are reborn many times and do not cease to exist at the point of physical death. For purposes of this book, I may choose to use the term "reincarnation" to mean "birth is not the beginning and death is not the end."

I've also learned in my studies that some souls often are reborn together for a variety of reasons. Sometimes, they have a very close bond and agree to reincarnate together. Often, our souls will change roles with those close to us sometimes being the parent and other times being the child. We always have free will to choose in the afterlife who or what we come back as, but it's also combined with lessons we must learn and karma we must settle and correct.

The proof that we do reincarnate and live many lives is laid out in books by Michael Newton, Ph.D., Brian Weiss, MD, Dr. Wayne Dyer, Edgar Cayce, and others, as well as the many books that explain the Akashic records. The books by these people prove beyond any doubt that we live on after this life, and then we come back again and again with many more lives until all of us reach our goal of soul perfection—all of us.

People say, "Why do bad things happen to good people?" and "Why would a loving God allow these tragedies to happen?" What I have learned is that there are no coincidences, and in our world, there is a great amount of synchronicity. This world we are in right now doesn't consist of randomness. It consists of a thorough plan to move each soul toward love. By not knowing this truth, it takes us longer to get there. Reading and understanding the material about reincarnation has helped me to speed up my evolution toward love, using my free will to live a more purposeful and satisfying life.

The next time you are asking yourself, "What is the point of my life?" consider the lessons discussed in this book. If I think about them, they make so much more sense than any other reason to be here now. Reincarnation or rebirth makes complete sense if you think about having to learn lessons and evolve toward love. How many people do you know that have done that in just their one lifetime? I don't know of anyone except maybe Jesus.

Whether it's jealousy, insecurity, greed, anxiety, violence, ego selfishness, being mean to animals, or any one of the many human foibles, we are on this planet to overcome and correct these faults with the lessons and opportunities presented to us. If we don't correct them, the lessons will be presented again differently and sometimes more harshly than before. That is until we have truly and completely corrected them.

How about the people who love money more than their fellow man? They don't die with a smile because, throughout their lives, they have never had enough of it. Do you think at the point of death, they finally realize that now they have exactly enough money? What about using this lifetime to break cycles of conflict, hatred, or violence? These are lessons we are all confronted with at some point.

Before my studies, I believed that karma was simply wishful thinking from people who were casting judgments on others. "Karma's a bitch" they defiantly pronounce. Karma is going to get them, is another common proclamation on those we judge as wrong. I've learned that all of us have karmic debts to work through and we knew what they were before we were reborn. The gentle voice of the holy spirit in our mind often reminds us of them when we choose to quiet the ego and listen to the spirit. I try to do this often because I take great comfort in paying these debts off, one at a time. I want to finish this life debt-free if possible. And these debts have nothing to do with money but everything to do with those people and animals I have hurt.

I learned that we take on different roles, genders, sexual orientations, cultures, races, and religions throughout our many lives. All of this is designed perfectly to teach us tolerance in this judgmental and vicious world. But it's only judgmental and vicious if I'm judgmental and vicious, so I've stopped being that. Once we die and go to the other side, there is no judgmental and vicious behavior -- only guiding, loving behavior. Imagine if we could bring that aspect of the afterlife to this world now. I think we can and I'm working on doing that in my orbit, one situation and one moment at a time.

Dr. Martin Luther King said, "The arc of the universe is long, but it bends toward justice." Well, I want to shorten that arc and bend myself toward justice now, today.

While I have been studying and learning throughout my life's journey and seeking the reason for this tour of duty, I have come across the truths laid out in this book. We are eternal and live many lives to learn love, forgiveness, and surrender. We are not judged harshly if we don't succeed but instead guided gently through other lives and into eternity until we get there. Through our many lives, we will get there, and as *A Course in Miracles* states, the outcome is not in doubt. The harsh events we have to endure are always lessons to bring us toward love. It is said that we grow the most through pain, but I don't want to have to endure that. I want to figure it out and grow through happiness, love, and surrender. Whenever I act now toward another living thing, I do it without condition. I do it because it makes me happy. Actively choosing this is self-fulfilling and builds confidence in my soul that I am on the right path.

We are all reborn many times and it's always to become a more perfect soul. The concept of reincarnation changed the way I looked at everything in my life. When I figured out the purpose for living many lives, it changed my life for the better because now I had a plan. No longer would I simply act out of selfishness or ignorance, but only out of working toward achieving something so much greater than myself. That's true empowerment.

> We all live multiple lives and the proof
> is there if you wish to find it.

Chapter 3

The Treasures of the Flesh

What can our bodies do after our souls have left it?

I know some of the most beautiful people in the world, and none of them would say they are happy with their bodies. Whenever they do something to make themselves more beautiful, they always have a list of more things that they want fixed next.

My friend Rebecca is a perfect example. And when I say perfect, I mean perfect. Rebecca is drop-dead gorgeous, and if I looked at her for a million years, I couldn't find a flaw...oh, yeah, except that in a million years, Rebecca's body will be nothing but atoms scattered around the universe. Maybe that will be beautiful, too. I don't know.

Rebecca is about as far from low-maintenance as a woman can get. She pays for eyelashes, eyebrows, hair extensions, balayage, nails -- beyond that, only she knows how much work she's had done. Yet when I see her, she always has some complaint about her physical appearance.

I love Rebecca. I love to be around her. I love looking at her -- sure I do. Enough to make me wonder, would I love her just as much if she looked a little less perfect? How about a lot less perfect? How about no teeth, a big old wart on her nose, and a hundred pounds of cellulite?

The truth is Rebecca's spirit is as beautiful as her physical form -- more beautiful because it has been and always will be just as pure, loving, and selfless as she is. But if I hadn't been initially attracted to her beauty, I admit I may never have gotten to know her eternal spirit.

Most of us have a complicated relationship with beauty and with our bodies because we are immortal beings having a human experience. As humans, we live in these rental car bodies, and our bodies have agendas of their own. Sometimes, it seems as if our bodies control our minds and not the other way around. The control comes about through insecurities that we must learn to vanquish.

When I realized I loved Rebecca -- the real, eternal Rebecca, not the rental car -- I started to wonder how much suffering I'd caused myself and others by my focus on the physical, impermanent beauty of the body rather than the eternal beauty of the spirit. I should have known better! I already understood that we were eternal, that we all outlive our bodies. And I'd already learned to focus on my own internal feelings of peace or conflict to tell me what was true and what was a lie I'd been conditioned to believe.

So, I started paying attention. And I found that our bodies bring us little joy and much more angst. Wishing I had more muscle or less fat or a bigger dick only served to make me less happy, whereas accepting what is, made me happier.

I have a friend who has enough nose hair protruding from his nostrils that it looks like two little hand brooms. Instead of focusing on his spirit, I can't stop looking at those sweepers. Identification with our bodies will always create a significant degree of dissatisfaction internally. That is, until we accept the impermanence and irrelevance of it.

It's hard to see the body as irrelevant in this culture. The human body is simultaneously exalted and worshipped as an object of beauty and reviled as a source of so-called sin. Think about how many people are appalled at the sight of nudity. People would lose their fucking minds if I walked around in public naked, and not because I'm the second coming of Adonis. Has all that vigilance against parts of our body made us more secure or more insecure?

Making friends with your human body -- and with everyone else's very human bodies -- without identifying them as "me/mine" or "they/theirs" is one of the hardest tasks of a well-lived spiritual life. But it's exactly what we need to do because second only to a fear of death, our love-hate relationship with our bodies causes more internal conflict and misery than just about anything.

I once got a fortune cookie that was so true that I couldn't forget it: If strength were all, the lion would not fear the scorpion.

I know a lot of men who train their bodies to be able to engage in a physical battle with another person and beat them. Rarely have I known any of them not to seek some sort of combat. That's what we train our children for. Almost one in five women in our culture have been raped, and not by other women. The largest majority of serial killers are men. According to the Huff Post, 85% of domestic violence victims are women, while almost double the number of women were killed in domestic violence between 2001 and 2012 than soldiers who were killed in Afghanistan in that same period. What are we teaching our men, our trained, home-grown combatants, to behave like?

I was trained to be a physically strong warrior and it took me many years to realize that it was not right for me. And I had to figure it out myself. None of my "spiritual" advisors ever brought it up because they were proud that I was a "good" soldier for our society. I was encouraged to enlist to go fight in Vietnam when I was younger, but I knew in my heart that I was going to get a Canadian forwarding address.

I have learned that the world needs fewer attackers and defenders, so I elected to give this world one less fighting man. Women are trained to be sexy but not sexual, smart but not smarter than the men, and support the war effort with their children. We train our bodies and minds for battle and use our bodies to carry it out. If the only thing that lives on after this short life is our soul, why do we continue to give such importance to our body and its desire to be attack-ready?

The amount of time I used to spend thinking about my body is significant. I still buy clothes and trinkets that I think make me look better. I still have a list of shit I want done to my body. Drop some weight in my stomach area but add muscle everywhere else, tighten my abs, butt lift, facelift, more tattoos, more hair on my head but less in my ears, fewer wrinkles, mani-pedi, eyelashes, plane my feet so they are perfect, bigger lips, tummy tuck, more piercings, Lasik surgery, tanning, dye my hair, and cut it too. Some of the bodily enhancements now seem a bit frivolous and unnecessary, so I put those on the "B" list.

I can make parts of my body more satisfactory, but it's an exhausting commitment. Kind of like mowing my lawn. I love it once I'm done, but I know I have to do it all over again in a week. It starts to annoy me.

What can my body do once my spirit leaves it? Nothing. Only decay. Yet, for much of my life, most of my thinking has revolved around my body. Cleaning, grooming, primping, bathing, plucking, trimming, shaving, coloring, eating, walking, running, lifting, dressing, and shitting, every single day, and I'm just getting started.

My body can't taste, smell, hear, see, or feel without my spirit, yet I have been conditioned to pamper, adorn, and glorify my body -- not my spirit. I identify much more with this temporary body rental than I identify with my spirit or true self. I wouldn't wash and vacuum a rental car. What do I keep when my short life is finished? It's not my body. My body is a vehicle to be used as an avenue of awareness and to communicate with other souls. Apart from my mind, my body has no purpose at all and can do nothing on its own without me.

When I started realizing that my body is largely insignificant in the scheme of eternity, how did it change me? I didn't stop working out, getting Brotox, shaving, or showering because it was way too ingrained in me to "look good." I admit I am a vain motherfucker.

Then I realized that my mind can heal my body, but my body can't heal my mind. My mind is much more powerful than my body. Working on only improving my body is like running after a person I can never catch. Understanding that my body is temporary has allowed me to put less emotional importance on how my body looks.

As I started seeking confirmation for this new release from hyper-focus on the physical, I discovered even more confirming truths.

1. Our current bodies are impermanent. Aside from preventative maintenance, what's the point?

2. The mind can heal the body, but the body can't heal the mind.

3. Phantom limb pain is a real thing because it is real to the mind.

4. The "placebo effect" consistently occurs in 21%–40% of people who heal themselves because they believe they have been given a cure, although it's only a sugar pill. When it comes to depression, studies have shown that placebos are more effective than the top 3 prescribed medications.

5. It is now more accepted that our brains don't create our thoughts, and our minds are far more extensive than our physical brains can contain. Many documented instances have shown that people who didn't have a functioning brain were conscious and lucid.

This knowledge means there is a whole way of thinking that I had not been previously taught. Why don't we teach about the power of the mind over the body? Instead, we have snake oil and prescriptions because it's profitable to sell remedies for our afflictions. I can pee better if I take saw palmetto, have a harder erection if I buy horny goat weed, and shit better if I eat plant fiber; different concoctions help with anxiety, depression, and stress. I've tried them all. But the one thing that always works is when I decide to make a change in my mind. That's where we should look for healing.

Clearly, the mind is far more powerful than the body. Taking care of our bodies is important, but not more important than taking care of our minds and spirits.

Does this mean that skin color, hair, looks, and body type don't matter? It does matter in this world, but not the next. Our bodies are used for the sole purpose of joining minds together and uniting each other in this life.

Even if I spent tons of time and treasure making myself look a certain way, I have no control over what will happen to my body when I walk out the front door, much less years from now when the effects of aging start to set in. I'm now convinced that, since there are some things I have no control over, I will stop spending time worrying about them.

According to past life regressions and LBLs, once we die, our bodies have zero importance in the spirit world, as we are pure energy. I've learned that we did choose the bodies we currently have, and this choice was part of the lessons we must learn in this lifetime. One example was a person who, in a previous life, had a big, strong male body and used it to impose his will on others in a physical manner. In his next life, he was given a small and weak body, and others imposed their will on him. I certainly don't want to have to learn those lessons again. Although with my current body, I could be a bully, and I probably was at earlier points in my life, I'm over it. No need for me to be oppressed throughout a lifetime by oppressing others now. Uncle. Love wins. Now when I lift weights it's so I can more easily lift my suitcase or stack wood. Not so that I can intimidate or physically impose myself on anyone or anything.

> We are not our bodies, and our bodies can do nothing without our spirits in them.

Chapter 4

Might as Well Face It:
I'm Addicted to Love

What daily thought processes are your addictions?

Whuhen I was running a business, sitting on four different non-profit Boards, and working bell to bell every day, I was addicted to painkillers. I started taking opiates when the internet became a common thing, and I could buy as many as I wanted simply by placing an order online. Within 18 months, these online drug marts would get shut down, so I had to find dealers. Here I was, a pillar of the community, hooked on the pill form of heroin. During the time I was a junkie, I was honored with Small Business Person of the Year and Good Samaritan of the Year, among other community awards—if only they knew.

My predisposition to addiction began when I was 15 years old. I started smoking cigarettes and weed and drinking. It was the only way I felt that I could advocate against the bald-faced hypocrisy and lying I was being indoctrinated with and rebel against "the man." And I was the poster child for rebellion because I was the quarterback of my high school football team, a good student, the star pitcher on the baseball team, and all the while, I was getting fucked up at every chance I could. One of my jobs at this time was driving a school bus in Newark, NJ, and I would go to the job at 6 AM, get high, and drive children. I was committed to never screwing up the whole while I was getting fucked up, and I always felt like I could control the addictions, as well as the high.

Then I went away to college and had access to the finest drugs available: weed, coke, PCP, crystal meth, acid, speed, Quaaludes, mushrooms and even heroin. I never turned down an opportunity to partake, but I also never lost control of my senses over drugs because I was confident that I was stronger than the drugs.

Why did I start doing harder drugs? First of all, those drugs almost always make you feel good...for a minute. And I was always looking for a more sincere way to be happy and connected to this life. Many drugs do that to a person until you build a tolerance and need more to get a similar feeling. This went on for over a decade until I finally decided that I'd had enough.

Addiction consumed my life; always counting my pills and figuring out when I would have to buy more. That meant getting cash and dealing with the unsavory people who could provide these illegal drugs. Because I had to be on my game every day, going through withdrawals wasn't an option. Going cold turkey from the level of opiate addiction I had meant feeling like shit for four to six weeks and having no energy.

Even though I finally got the monkey off my back with opiates, I realized that I was addicted to much more than just pills. Nicotine, caffeine, making money, trying to win all the battles, pretty women, gaining acceptance by others, fast cars, gambling, and much more. Eventually, I realized that all of my addictions were really a search for love and meaning in my life.

When any of us devote ourselves habitually to any thought patterns or pursuits, we are addicted. Addiction in any form is our way of giving up our sacred power of living consciously because the addiction becomes our daily priority. I gave up my most powerful addictions because I learned that they would never get me where I wanted to go, and my worst addictions were my own thought patterns.

I became addicted because I believed that I was lacking things that my addiction would provide. Peace, safety, health, excitement, love, and joy were all states of being that I was seeking through external means. As I continued my evolution, I learned that there is never anything outside of me that gives me long-term happiness, love, and joy. Think about that -- we always search for things outside of ourselves that will make us more complete, but never do we find them. The power of completeness resides only in our minds and always has.

I now know and identify what my addictions are, and I don't punish myself for having them. I have just decided that if these habits bring me happiness and joy, I can decide to keep them -- or not. This learning and growth helped me relinquish most all addictions, especially those that kept me in mental bondage. Everything else I do because I choose to, and doing so brings me chronic happiness. But they are not habits anymore. Now, they are conscious decisions, and that frees me.

According to the Orlando Recovery Center, the four stages of addiction are:

- Experimentation: uses or engages out of curiosity
- Social or regular: uses or engages in social situations or for social reasons
- Problem or risk: uses or engages extremely with disregard for consequences

- Dependency: uses or engages in behavior daily, or several times per day, despite possible negative consequences

Based on these stages, I can draw the similarity to many behaviors, not just drug use. For example, let's say that we give up our freedom of thought and free will to religious, cultural, or political dogma. This conditioning and indoctrination acts as a filter blocking the true meaning of what we are supposed to do in this life on Earth. It feeds a state of constant pursuit of individual greatness and selfishness versus the betterment of all souls as equals. Deep down, we know that the latter is the true goal, and this causes guilt and angst.

Once I relinquished most of my addictions, getting rid of these attachments became a victory and a strong desire in my life. I still sometimes get fucked up and do drugs, but I no longer need it or allow it to control my behavior. This comes from my desire to no longer escape from life, except for the occasional night, because I no longer allow this life to beat me down. I have learned and practiced strategies for healing that work for me now that don't include constant and chronic addictions.

Despite my addictions to chemicals and drugs, I have found it even more difficult to break the thought patterns that have controlled my life for as long as I can remember. These are even more destructive than any drug and way more persistent. Almost all of these thought patterns emanate from my past, which is unchangeable and irrelevant, except as lessons I had to learn. I always say that I have an angel on my right shoulder and an asshole on my left. The one that influences me is the one I feed.

In an attempt to control the world around us, we mentally create models for ourselves and others. We believe that these mental confinements will, in some way, make us safer, allow us to predict the future better, and reduce

the randomness of our lives. We create roles and rules of expected be.
and when others don't conform, we judge harshly. These mental boundaries are like invisible fences around our heads and become another form of addictive thinking until we become aware of them and understand they are of no value because they fictionally impose limitations on our glorious existence. I can say that I'm a man, or a business owner, or a father, or a white American, but I don't have to accept society's script written for that role.

If you're not genuinely happy with life, I recommend that you examine the roles and related behavior you have created around those roles. Those are the addictions and habits that you should consider breaking, and as *A Course in Miracles* teaches, there is no order of difficulty in changing your mind. The difficulty is always at the same level when it comes to mental and spiritual growth.

I'm not saying that having basic behavioral expectations isn't good. However, expanding them to daily roles and relationships misses the point of giving up past thinking processes and simply enjoying the now. Often, these addictive thought processes manifest into something like this: a person close to you behaves in a way that you don't like, so you tell your friends about it. Then, it becomes a whole event of negativity whereby your friends confirm your feelings and share similar stories with the group. The negativity abounds and nothing is accomplished. You may feel better for a short period, but that is fleeting. Now, when others try to drag me into their drama, I tell them that I don't want to entertain the negativity because if I do, I make it real. And it's not real because it is only a temporary judgment that proves nothing. I have found that a lot fewer people seek me out to just complain about life stuff now because they don't like me as an audience for that type of conversation. I'm good with that.

Another common mental addiction is that of never giving ground on things you think you want, whether material things or relationship things. I've been in relationships with people who get angry if I don't want the same thing for dinner they want, or I don't want to work out when they want, or other mundane, irrelevant conflicts. I won't relinquish anything I believe in, such as honesty, peace, love, and other soulful pursuits, but I no longer impose any of my beliefs on others. I feel like the best way I can improve the world is by being a model for others to follow. Or they don't have to follow my lead since it's beyond my control.

I have traveled the world and met people of all different cultures and backgrounds, and the one thing I can tell you is that we are all the same. The real addiction we all have in humanity is the addiction to love and the connection to other souls. The problem is that we all think we know the way to achieve that, and so it becomes our addiction, even when the consequences are negative. I have found that the best way to achieve love and connection is to change my addictive thought processes away from conflict, separation, and judgment and only toward love. These addictive thought processes ruled my behavior for more years than I'd like to admit. Most of us wake up and live a semi-automatic life filled with conflict, judgments, bickering, and doing what we did yesterday and all the days before. I am now addicted to seeking peace and love and experiencing the new lessons the universe sends me, and I am always happy doing it.

> We are all addicted to something.
> Why not make it the best thing?

Chapter 5

Live Free or Die

Do we predominately use our present thinking or are we marionettes to conditioning, group thinking, and lies?

I live in a state where every license plate says, "Live Free or Die." I love the passion but hate the hypocrisy. Try not to pay a tax bill, license your dog, or go into a state park when it's not open, and you will quickly find that there's no truly <u>living free</u> here or anywhere on this planet. Yet we believe and kill for the belief that we have to protect our "freedoms."

According to a recent study based on the United Nation's Universal Declaration of Human Rights, the U.S. came in 52nd among all countries for being the freest. If "Freedom isn't Free," according to the old veteran's bumper sticker, what will it cost to get into the top ten? The only true freedom we all have as humans is our own free will. I guess freedom is free after all because our free will always originates at the thought level of our minds.

This is far from the "freedoms" we are taught we have to kill and die for. Are we still warring because we're not free from the British? How many of us died for our freedom in Korea? Vietnam? Iraq? Afghanistan? Those wars were not because of a threat to our freedom but more because they were a threat to our "interests." As Noam Chomsky, famed scholar and MIT professor, once said, "If we want to end terrorism throughout the world, we first should stop being the world's biggest terrorist." Since the end of World War II, the U.S. military has been directly responsible for the killing of over 20 million people.

The United States is the largest arms dealer in the world and from 2017 to 2021, it sold weapons to more than 100 countries. Ronald Reagan used to say that the U.S. will create "peace through strength," but has our mighty military strength created more peace or more war?

Studies comparing the results of non-violent civil disobedience versus armed conflict have shown that the former are twice as likely to achieve the desired goals of social change. They have also shown that those campaigns that have engaged at least 3.5% of the population have never failed to bring about change! Look at the research by Erica Chenoweth, a political scientist at Harvard University, that clearly shows that civil disobedience is the most powerful way of shaping world politics, as opposed to arming and warring.

The fact that everyone has free will is a powerful and often unspoken truth. Everyone on this planet has the same free will. We are all born with this as factory-installed, standard equipment. We can choose not to use it, but we all get it. Free will. Do what I want. Think how I want, not spastic, involuntary, and uncontrollable behavior and thoughts. Think and do as I choose.

When I was a kid, it was my stepdad's one great project to try to squash my free will. That's not his fault. He was raised to think that was a father's job. His father did it to him, too.

When I realized I was doing the same goddamned thing to my wife and kids, that's when things started changing for me. That time I got so pissed off at my son when he threw his plate on the floor didn't have anything to do with the mess it made -- or not much, anyway. A mess I could clean up in a few minutes. The way my kid cried when I yelled at him hit me in a much more lasting way. And why did I yell, anyway? Because I was angry, yeah. Like I said before, I was always angry back then. But that <u>particular</u> time, my pretext for anger was that the little fucker wouldn't eat his vegetables when I told him to.

I say "pretext" because that's all it was. Deep down, I wasn't just angry. I was scared to death. Here was this kid I'd participated in making, and <u>I couldn't do a damn thing to control him</u>. Not outside of physical violence, anyway, and after the way my stepdad used to treat me, I'd promised myself I'd never go down that route.

Why do we get mad and scared and try to take away one another's free will? I think it's because we're afraid we'll be left alone if we let go of control over others. But in fact, the opposite is true. We push people away -- and have less control over them -- when we try to rob them of their free will. Whenever we try to control others, they feel constrained and we get frustrated. Whenever I have attempted to control another person's behavior, they may seem like they are being compliant, but what they are really doing is hiding that behavior that I discouraged from me. My attempts at control are temporary and impotent. It drives people away from me and me away from them. It never ends well.

Until I considered the absolute power of free will, my thoughts and behavior were mostly automatic reactions to what or who was in front of me. I realized that much of the time, I was acting based on semi-automatic reactive behavior and not on a full understanding of the power that true free will endowed me with. If someone said to me, "Fuck you!" I quickly countered with the insightful and brilliant comeback of, "Fuck you, too!"

My automatic behavior wasn't keeping me from doing most things that I wanted to do, but I knew that I wanted less conflict and more happiness in my life. I started considering how society and culture teach freedom as a physical state, but a more powerful and permanent freedom is that of the mind. I decided that I was going to use my will to eliminate everything in my life that didn't bring me joy, happiness, or the outcomes I desired.

I quickly learned that this was going to be a practice and not a light switch since so much of my stress or inner conflict was an almost automatic reaction to situations and people I was surrounded by. People still pissed me off, not being able to talk to a real person when I had a problem pissed me off, clueless drivers pissed me off, and sometimes (still!) everything pissed me off. As I began observing what was keeping me from being happy all the time, I realized there was a long list of offenders, and I thought it was my job to change them.

My parents pissed me off, as did my co-workers. Banks pissed me off, spam pissed me off, my friends pissed me off, and incompetent road planners got me going. Politicians, holy men, hypocrites, warriors, lawyers, liars, controlling women, and even my kids all pissed me off. Not to where I overtly displayed this anger anymore like I used to, but inside my mind, I was angry or annoyed. Not happy.

Then I had an <u>aha</u> moment. All these times I got mad never changed a single situation for the better. I couldn't even remember all the times I got mad just yesterday, so what was the point of all that futile anger? Getting annoyed or mad no longer had any value for the new, happier me. More and more as I stopped reacting emotionally to daily situations, I started feeling freer. I no longer cared about what people say or don't say. I began to see the world around me in a much more objective way, now knowing that nothing could keep me from being happier unless I alone allowed it. I realized that chronic happiness is not just an emotion; it's a decision. I have a choice of being happy or not, and I realized that my level of happiness is completely independent of the acts, omissions, or thoughts of other people. Live free or die trying.

My anger in the past wasn't wrong; it simply no longer expresses who I am today. I use my free will to reconsider how I view my past. I can't change the past, but I can use my will to stop it from hurting me now. I was taught to "suck it up," "don't be a pussy," and to "be a man" when things didn't go well. In other words, get pleasure out of the pain in life rather than learn how to eliminate the pain in life. Getting some stupid pleasure out of the pain simply kept me in the constant pain loop while eliminating it is final and complete.

I could no longer deceive myself into believing I was helpless in the face of what was done to me. This realization came along with another: I can't have a feeling I don't choose. Not for very long, anyway. Feelings will always come, but they're temporary -- very temporary, if you let them be. Unless you choose to hold onto a feeling (consciously or unconsciously), it can't become part of your state of being. So, I began to consciously choose happiness. After years of making this choice, I no longer have to do it consciously, as it has become my semi-automatic reaction to virtually every situation that used to aggravate and anger me.

I have learned that once I decided that I was going to be happy from this day forward, I can be. There will be situations and people that test my resolve, but being confident that I have all the power to overcome these makes it much quicker and easier to let things go.

It's not form or bondage that I seek, yet that is exactly what I allowed my education and culture to shackle me with for most of my life. The rules and mores, the judgments and biases, the group think and my non-think, each was another restriction to my free thinking and will. I knew that this was making my soul smaller and less free. I determined that the most effective way to stop all the conflict was first to ask myself what I wanted the outcome of every situation to be. Whether I was seeing familiar people or meeting new people, I would quickly consider how I wanted the meeting to end and then channeled all my energy into getting that desired outcome without regard for how the other person behaved. Now I know that it is only me I can control, so trying to control or wish others would behave in a certain way is no longer an extension of me.

If only we were taught about this amazing power when we were young! Imagine how much anxiety and depression we could avoid, not only our own but also all of the negativity we perpetrated on others with our controlling madness.

My spirit recoils when someone tries to restrain my free will or tell me what to do. In identifying this feeling in myself, I have learned not to attempt to judge or control other people's free will and behavior. It is me who has been set free.

We all have free will to see people and events however we choose.

Choosing conflict is chronic and perpetual.

Choosing peace is eternal and final.

Chapter 6

Surrender, but Don't Give Yourself Away

We are taught never to surrender, but learning the right way to do it is the key to eternal happiness.

I've mentioned "surrender" a few times, and it's an important concept in creating a happy life, perhaps one of the top three most important, along with being self-aware and eliminating my own ego. I'm not talking about unconditional surrender, whereby your fate is now in the hands of other people. It's not about waving a white flag with your hands up in the air. What I'm promoting that has been the most difficult practice in my life is to stop fighting everyone and everything in your mind. Surrender to giving a shit about what other people do, think, or say unless what they are doing or saying is important to you.

This is significant because if you don't, you keep yourself in constant battle. Battle-ready, battle-tested, battle-tough. A warrior waiting for their next challenge. And none of this makes you any stronger, tougher, or safer. It does exactly the opposite.

Men are trained to be strong and physical, and this has been successful because we live in a male-dominated society, and us guys aren't going to give up that supremacy easily. The newest term for this is toxic masculinity and males in many cultures are just that -- toxic. Not bad humans, merely toxic to peace and still running this war-plagued world.

According to representwomen.org, as of June 2022, there are 147 (28%) women in Congress: 24 in the Senate and 123 in the House. In 333 statewide elective executive offices, 101 (30%) are either led or co-led by women. Of 7,383 seats in state legislatures, women hold 2,295 (31%). At the local level, 367 (25%) of 1,465 cities are represented by women, and 80 (33%) of the five largest county governments in each state are either led or co-led by women.

We still have never seen a woman President. It was just over 100 years ago that women gained the right to vote because before that, women were seen as childlike and incapable of independent thought, and most men believed they couldn't be trusted to vote responsibly.

I would contend that our society is so male-dominated that individual and collective physical force is seen as the most important attribute, if not overtly, but certainly covertly. 80% of our military is male and an even higher percentage of the officers are male. Women run less than 11% of the Fortune 500 companies. Today, women earn 82 cents for every dollar a man makes in the same job and it gets even worse if you are a black or Hispanic woman. As someone who hired many people over the years, I can tell you that there's no good reason for this.

I could go on and on about this, but in our culture, we are male-trait dominated from birth and throughout our school years. This cultural conditioning is exemplified by men being physically strong and emotionally hardened. I was brought up to reject the "female" traits such as being gentle, emotional, and less competitive. Surrendering even one inch of ground in any situation was seen as weak, "gay," and a losing position.

But one day, the thought hit me: if I didn't fight back, wasn't that a stronger position to take than merely reacting to a challenge with a return challenge? Of course, it was because it took more restraint and intelligence. I remember one night in a bar, I went up to a table of four attractive women who were having a drink. I said politely, "Excuse me, but could I buy you ladies a drink?" One of the women immediately looked at me with anger and said, "Fuck off, Grandpa." In my earlier years, I would have come back with a rude comment that had the words "fucking bitch" in it. Still, because I was practicing being a scientific observer and not allowing my emotions to enter into any interactions through surrendering to what was, I simply smiled and replied, "That is an interesting response to an unconditional and friendly offer." Two of the women began laughing. We ended up having a good conversation together. I think the night turned out to be fun because, in my state of surrender, I was not seen as a threat.

The power of my learning surrender cannot be overstated. Surrender can be practiced in every situation that causes any emotion, especially anger, angst, frustration, depression, or any other negative feeling. I'm not succumbing to and accepting that feeling, but instead, I'm surrendering to the peace and love in my heart. I am releasing my attachment to the negativity and surrendering to what the universe will show me next.

I used to get mad at drivers who would get into the fast lane on the highway and not move over. I would flash my high beams at them, get about an inch from their bumper, and even periodically engage my horn. I even thought about getting air horns so I could make those bad drivers shit their pants. A few years ago, I decided I would send focused mental energy to the back of their heads, asking politely, "Please move over, please move over." I started noticing that more of them seemed to comply with my requests. Then I brought a pad of paper with me that had four columns -- one was people who moved over when I didn't think any thoughts, and the next was those who didn't when I had no thoughts. The third column was people who moved over when I mentally asked politely, and the last were those who didn't move over when I asked telepathically (either unaware or assholes). What I found in an admittedly non-scientific study was that my focused energy request was much more successful than not. I would even say that it was statistically significant. The only variations I didn't test for were all those years I became enraged when people didn't move over, but now, instead of getting angry and upset, I was having fun. For those people who ignored me, they were no longer assholes but now merely a mark in a column of my study -- a simple statistic. I surrendered my anger and road rage by consciously interacting with it in the moment.

Other situations that used to upset me are now met with surrender. There were times that I would text another person and wait impatiently for their response. If it didn't come, I would get annoyed or start thinking bad thoughts about what that person was doing. Now I text people because I want to send them a communication. They are under no obligation to respond or reply -- I sent that text because it made me feel good. When I help someone out, I go through the same thought process. They owe me nothing; I did this because it made me feel good, not because I expected anything in return.

When I get stressed about money now, I surrender my stress to the fact that whether I'm calm or stressed, the issue is exactly the same. Internal stress won't increase my bank account, but calmly thinking of solutions or considering what's the worst that can happen if I don't get more redirects my thoughts to a better line of thinking.

When I surrender my desire to control others or give up my judgmental thoughts, I am immediately put at peace. If I am sick, I surrender to the universe, knowing that aside from taking some medicine that may or may not work, I have no control anyway. Many spiritual healers work that way, too. I've read many books on spiritual healing. Although I am not here to give medical advice to anyone, it seems as though surrendering to the universe mixed with loving energy is the key to healing without medicine or when all other avenues have failed.

When I invoke surrender to forgive everyone that I have past anger for, my life becomes immediately lighter. When I realized that my past learning had brought me to a place of constant conflict and unhappiness, I surrendered to the thought process that I knew nothing about what was right from my past conditioning and resultant addictive thought patterns.

Learning to surrender wasn't easy or quick for me, and after three decades of recognizing the importance of it, I still am a work in progress. I still have moments when I forget my lessons of the past, but now I immediately recognize those moments and can talk myself down. If there are people in my life who continuously raise my hackles, I communicate with them less. When I do have to communicate with them, I decide the outcome I want before meeting with them and think in a way that achieves that desired outcome. For example, I will convince myself that I want both of us not to argue or debate and to have a happy and enjoyable interaction. I will even extend loving energy from my heart out to them throughout the meeting.

I have learned that surrender isn't a weakness, but it is a great strength. Ask anyone who knows me and they all marvel at the charisma and confidence I exude even though, in my own mind, I may be struggling slightly. I think almost everyone I know would love to be calmer and more confident, but they won't find it in the attachments of this world. It can only be found in quiet places and mindful thinking in their mind. Turn down the volume of the ego and consider what you want for eternity. Then go make it happen.

> Surrender isn't a weakness, but it is one
> of the greatest strengths we can learn.

Chapter 7

The Ever-Changing Past

In eternity, how significant is your unique past? How much time do you waste thinking about it?

If you're like me, you think a lot about the past. For me, much of that thinking used to be related to events that hurt me -- either through other people's thoughts and deeds or situations that turned out poorly. Being a jealous asshole, stealing something, having another person call me "unfeeling and cold," and getting humiliated in front of my friends have all run through my mind more recently. I seemed to remember these events over and over, even reliving bad situations that occurred decades ago.

And I did some shit that "proper society" would never forgive me for. I was addicted to opiates for over ten years. I gambled to excess. I drank like a fish and then drove home. I spent a lot of money on women, bribed decision-makers to make more money, and licked the asses of white bankers to borrow more money than my financial statements supported. But it's all past now. Irrelevant. Unimportant. Yet, I still beat myself up for these times.

Consider this about our past: Two people at the same event remember it differently, so our past is unique to each one of us. All of us have cultural and conditioning filters and biases that affect our objectivity in all situations. Why do we put so much importance on our past, considering everyone else has their own private exclusive story? Recently, I was talking to an ex about a trip we took together. She recalled how it was the best time of her life, while I remember that trip, thinking that I couldn't get home fast enough to break up with her. I'm so glad she had fun.

Each of our unique pasts creates the "story" of who we are. We like or don't like parts of our "stories." Over time, we modify our stories to fit the narrative we want others to know about us and then that becomes our truth. How true is fiction? Is your story you? Mine isn't me. I'm not the same person I was back then. We cannot directly share with others our experiences, perceptions, and past because we are translating situations to another person, and they are using a different translator to interpret that "story."

Love, however, can be shared directly with others and requires no translation as it is a universal language. Are you still the same person from your storied past? It's frightening to give up our uniqueness and past -- until you start doing it. Then, it becomes empowering and promotes learning and growth. Being stuck in the past retards our growth and evolution. Constantly thinking about the past -- especially the bad times -- keeps hurting us over and over.

As I began releasing myself from my past, I was finally stopping the people who had hurt me from hurting me today, even though they had stopped hurting me years ago. I realized that my past traumas were creating today's dramas. I also started realizing that the past had no value to me anymore. When I let my past make me sad or angry, I realized that it was a past cause of today's effects. Once I decided not to give any power to the cause, the effects dissipated in direct proportion to the amount of power I gave them.

Learning this made me understand that I didn't have to give up my negative past or my glory days; I just had to stop believing that these stories continue to hold value now. Why is it still important that I beat up some guy or scored a touchdown? Why is it valuable that someone called me out in front of a group? It no longer mattered that I was addicted or failed at something. It only mattered what I thought and did next.

I started considering that my past was not a thousand individual events but more a continuous part of my eternal life. My past was a tapestry of lessons that fit together as a whole. It's like each of us has a singular, one-of-a-kind past that is designed as our personal course in evolution because no two pasts are the same. Even when I talk to my siblings about events that we all were present for, we each have a different perspective and remember different things about it -- homeschooling before homeschooling. I could take anyone of these situations and allow it to continue to impact my life today in a negative way even though it happened years ago. Even if it happened yesterday, it's still just as done.

When I was nine years old, I was walking home alone from school through the woods. Although I had only moved there a year before, it was an area I walked every day, played in, and loved. I came upon a bunch of boys who were much older than me in the middle of the forest and they started pushing me and hitting me. All of a sudden four boys each grabbed an arm and leg and started pulling me. I was powerless and scared. One of the bigger boys then pulled my pants and underwear down and, while I was being held on the ground, proceeded to anally rape me with a tree branch. Because I had been so terrorized physically by my stepdad, I didn't cry or show any pain, but I'm sure they knew I wasn't enjoying it. Once they saw my asshole starting to bleed, they laughed and let me go and left. I immediately stood up, got dressed, and walked home, trying to figure out if I should say anything to my parents. I knew if I told them, I would get in trouble for either walking home through the woods, not fighting them off, or ruining my underwear that now they would have to replace. So, I got home, went into the bathroom, washed, and wiped my ass. Then I went and threw out my underwear, hoping my stepdad didn't find it on garbage night. Fortunately for me, he didn't because if he had, I'm not sure my ass could endure another beating. I thought about it for a while, mostly afraid of being found out.

I periodically saw the boy who had done it to me in the neighborhood and I would avoid him at all costs. Fortunately, we moved away a short time later and I never told anyone what had happened. In a way, I forgave those boys almost immediately because I didn't want to relive the emasculation and helplessness I felt at that moment. I'm not saying it was the right choice, but I'm saying it was the choice I made. Forgive and forget. I didn't want to battle those boys anymore or my parents for the perceived infraction that I must have committed. Or I could simply keep battling individual people and situations until I win every single one, all the while creating a past, present, and future full of conflicts.

I know a person who was raped and stabbed by her stepfather when she was a teenager. Thirty years later, she still won't have intimate relationships and carries around that trauma as if it is a part of who she is. Once I said to her that although I could never understand the pain she went through, maybe she was allowing that man to do the same thing to her over and over. She agreed but she has to heal in her way and on her terms.

Studying past life regressions has taught me that we each are here in this moment to learn to evolve toward love. Our lives are a series of situational lessons designed to allow us to use our own free will to make better decisions. If we make the wrong decision in a given situation, the lesson will be presented differently...until we learn it. If we don't learn it in this life, there's always the next.

> Learning toward love is the only lesson we must learn from our past, so the curriculum is easy to learn. Maybe a bit harder to execute on, though, unless we are aware of our purpose.

I wanted to change the way my past was creating my present and future -- and stop it now. To better understand my life, I had to first consider that maybe all the events of my past weren't random occurrences happening to me but lessons meant to bring me closer to my eternal nature. There was nothing outside of myself creating my past, but only decisions I was making each day. I started to own my past, forgive myself for it, and take full accountability for the next moves. I had created everything in my mind up until now. My whole world was occurring in my mind alone. If I died, the entire thing would vanish -- my story of my past, my reactions in the present, my dreams of the future. All that would be left would be _me_ -- the one creating it all.

With that awareness, I now understood that I could craft my life's situational outcomes by figuring out what I wanted and work on creating it. That's a scary responsibility, but ultimately, I want it no other way. It's all on me.

I kept the happy memories and learned to redirect the negative thoughts immediately. The past no longer hurts me. Now, it heals me. Otherwise, I was punishing myself for crimes I never committed. Achieving growth was much more difficult if I remained fixated on yesterday's littleness. I was done allowing my past to define my present and shape my future. I was going to learn the lessons of yesterday and behave differently now to shape my future.

Everyone has heard the saying, "Those who don't study the past are condemned to repeat it!" But we <u>do</u> study the past constantly, and we still keep repeating it. We should change our curriculum because the cost of our ignorance is conflict, unhappiness, stress, depression, insecurity, and a lot less love.

We can't change the past, but most of us never stop trying to rewrite our stories in our minds.

> The past can only hurt us if we allow it.
>
> Giving up our fixations on the past is giving up nothing of value in the present.

Chapter 8

Whose Rules? What Game?

What are your rules and do they make sense if we are all connected and eternal?

As I began the formal journey of increasing my happiness and decreasing my conflict, it dawned on me that there are two distinct sets of rules. There are all the rules we know living in this material and physical world, and then there are rules of the spirit.

Rules of the spirit are different and almost always the opposite of the rules of the world, and we rarely stop to consider their contradictory positions in our lives. Unless and until we learn how to listen to the spirit, we may not even hear its voice. After all, the rules of the world are loud and in our faces.

- He who dies with the most toys wins.
- Second place is the first loser.
- Dying in a war for your country is honorable.
- The color of someone's skin defines them.
- Our history of terrorism and oppression of non-Americans have made us "great" and wealthy.

- Men are superior to women.
- People who are not heterosexual are abnormal and immoral.
- Some souls are lesser than others based on wealth.
- And on and on.

Go walk through a cemetery and you will see that some people must have been financially successful and think that when they die, the biggest monuments to their existence will get them more consideration in the afterlife. Yet, almost no one remembers them on Earth a few years after they are gone. That $50,000 headstone would have saved a lot of children and abused animals.

The teachers of this world have taught me that there's a heaven and hell, so I'd better not swear, desire to make love to my neighbor's wife, have more than one God other than the Gods of money, status, fame, power, judgment, and other temporary nonsense. I see us housing the elderly in institutions to prolong their life span, but aside from Friday Pizza at the old age home, not the quality.

Our spirit knows that our bodies are only temporary shells, yet the world puts incredibly irrelevant emphasis on its most insignificant attributes. I've spent more hours increasing the size of my biceps than I have on increasing the love in my soul. We can get face lifts, tummy tucks, butt lifts, skin tightening, tattoos, piercings, sex changes, new boobs, penis enlargement, hair removal and regrowth, and so much more, but we can't buy inner peace and soulfulness.

I can train my body to run further, lift heavier shit, be tighter, and feel better -- temporarily. Training my mind to be full of love and peace requires similar diligence and discipline, but the rewards are so much more long-lasting. If I do planks, crunches, thrusts, lunges, shrugs, clean and jerks, snatches, hops and chops, sit-ups, push-ups, pull-ups, chin-ups, step-ups, sleepers, jacks and jumps, I can change my body for a bit. If I practice forgiveness, amnesty, absolution, unconditionality, exoneration, and cancellation of all wrongs done to me, I change my outlook and soul forever.

The rules of this world teach us that we are all unique and separate individuals. That's not such a bad thing on the surface. After all, while we are here on Earth, it certainly seems to be the case. I'm over here in my meat suit; you're over there in yours.

The problem arises when we believe that our individuality is vital to our survival and more important than being connected to all living things at the universal energy level. Then, we learn that we have to fight to defend our individuality. This creates conflict in our relationships. If I'm out to "get mine," and you're out to get yours, I'm going to have to fight to control you to get what I think I want -- and you're going to have to do the same. No thanks.

The rules of the spirit teach us that we are each connected by living in this world at the same time. We come from the same eternal source, and we return to the same eternal source. We are here living temporarily, connected by our humanity, to evolve and increase the all-knowingness of the eternal. We are in it together. Doesn't that sound nicer than the illusion of separateness, of constant competition over apparently scarce resources?

The spirit can only be reached when each of us focuses on creating our better selves and letting others do the same. How can I teach peace if I'm not at peace within myself? How am I qualified to fix others if I'm not fixed? I'm like a shoe-shine boy with dirty shoes. We are all guilty of it -- telling people whom they shouldn't sleep with, what they shouldn't eat, how they shouldn't raise their kids. We all do it. If we don't say it, we think it. We can fix every human in our orbits except ourselves. That's because the world's judges are fallible, but the spirit doesn't judge -- it guides. I wish that fucking voice would shout at me sometimes, but it never does. So, we have to figure it out ourselves. Every one of us is on our own, so it seems from the physical world.

The good news is, deep down in the quiet of our mind, our inner spirit's voice knows the rules and teachings of the world can't be true. The world won't endure forever -- and we certainly won't endure forever in the world. If the rules and teachings of the world are no longer true after we die, why not stop believing them now?

If we listen, the rules of the spirit show us that we can think in whatever way we want to and react to any situation in any fashion that we want. The spirit teaches that we can live with peace and love toward all others and still attain exactly what we want without misery. The only caveat is that we have to <u>choose</u> to live this way. This is not the way we are taught, but those who learn it on their own live happier and more successful lives.

The rules of the world defend and protect our egos; the person we portray but aren't. It's the persona we have created as we have grown up in this world. The ego consists of our bodies, our non-spiritual past, the roles we have accepted and live within, and the person we think we are when living without self-awareness. Our egos account for all unhappiness, all feelings of lack, all wars, all violence, all hatred, and all insecurity. The ego always identifies us with the material form -- physical, status, financial, or any other earthly impermanent forms. When I read Eckhart Tolle's description of the ego as the "collective human dysfunction," I knew he had nailed it. But our egos don't live on beyond this lifetime because they are irrelevant in eternity. So why do we give such loyalty to a made-up construct such as the ego? Because we are not taught that we aren't a tiny individual against the universe but we are a part of this wonderful, connected plan toward love. The ego only has as much power over us as we are willing to give allegiance to it. Our egos don't want us to know the truth because when we do, the ego won't have any place or power within us. Our egos make us believe that without it, the world will be full of conflict, chaos, and hatred. But don't we have that now, as we have allowed our egos to lead us?

The spirit doesn't yell, promote, or debate but gently reminds us who we are -- a loving and peaceful eternal soul. We always hear the ego in our minds because the ego always speaks first, but we rarely take the time to listen to the spirit because it speaks much more softly, not selling or oppressing. Just knowing. That's because it knows that the ego isn't real and eternal, but the spirit is. The spirit knows we will get back to it and listen once this life is done, but I'm not waiting to die to learn to live in peace now.

We all want inner peace and joy -- all the time. The world of the ego makes us believe that we have to fight for it. Win all the battles and the spoils of war will be ours. Most of the lessons we learn in school confirm this. Most of our statues and heroes won battles so we all could have freedom, a big land mass, and bragging rights. We beat the Native Americans, Africans, Mexicans, Japanese, French, Spanish, British, Germans, Italians, South Americans, and even our southern brothers and sisters. The only people we didn't slaughter were the Canadians -- because they won't fight back and Canada is too freaking cold!

In reality, there are only two ways of thinking. The first is thinking with the ego and the second is thinking with the spirit. It's very simple. When you choose the ego, you get chaos, conflict, and pain. When you choose the spirit, you get peace, love, and joy. I have learned that if I want to become more soulful and at peace, I have to identify the barriers that keep me from thinking with the spirit and, one by one, dissolve them into yesterday. Once they are gone, I never have to deal with them again. Eliminating my ego has become one of my foremost and important practices. It's the most valuable and worthwhile endeavor I can undertake.

These days, I often look at the rules of the world and decide if I wish to comply with them. It makes me happy to have that power of free will. Do I want to drive the speed limit? Smoke weed? Pay my bills? Sleep around? Fart in a crowded elevator? Will doing so increase my happiness and peace or put me more deeply into conflict? The answer is usually quite simple -- though not always easy.

Unlike the rules of the world, the rules of the spirit aren't many, but sometimes it's difficult to learn what they are. The physical world is much louder in its persistent assertions. I've had to consciously decide to start listening more deeply and questioning which makes me happier -- listening to the voice of the spirit or the voice of my ego. As I learn the spirit, I have learned that it is possible to follow its laws and live in relative harmony with the world's laws -- by my own choice. As long as I choose peace and happiness, I am a shitload happier.

> There are rules of this physical world and rules of the spirit.
> Only the rules of the spirit make any sense in eternity.

In this world, our egos are loud and prominent but cease to exist when we leave this life.

Chapter 9

Never Enough

What is it that your soul needs right now to be happy besides your decision?

I know a woman who was raised by her parents to live in constant competition with her older sister. In her house, love and attention were a scarce resource, and there was never enough to go around. When they were young, the two sisters were forced to compete over who would get the most praise for being smarter, more athletic, a better musician, or a better mirror for whatever their parents secretly felt they should have been, to earn their own parents' affection. (This shit gets passed down through generations.)

When the sisters became teenagers, the older one developed the skill of getting all the attention by acting out. Her big trick was to put her life in danger (risky sex, drugs, driving drunk, self-harm, suicide attempts) so her parents would be terrified into coming to her rescue. Pretty clever.

Meanwhile, the younger sister quietly learned to live without love or attention. As a result, when she became an adult, she always felt a sense of emptiness inside her. For a while, she tried to fill it up with the same garbage as her sister -- risky sex, drugs, driving drunk, self-harm, suicide attempts.

But she was in her twenties by then and estranged from her parents, so no one came to her rescue. This was the best thing that could have happened because she had to rescue herself. For a while, she developed a habit of pulling what recovering alcoholics call "a geographical cure." She moved all over the country and then all over the world, trying to save herself.

As the saying goes, "Wherever you go, there you are."

She couldn't outrun that empty place inside her. But that empty place was about to become the thing that finally saved her.

When I met her, this woman told me a story about something that happened to her when she moved to Japan to teach English to middle school students. It was winter vacation, and she was bitterly miserable and lonely in a country where she didn't speak the language well and had no friends. On a whim, she decided to visit a Buddhist monastery she'd read about in a guidebook. She knew just enough Japanese to say "yes" when a monk asked her if she wanted to learn how to sit zazen -- that is, Zen meditation.

She followed the monk down a wooden path through a snowy garden into a huge, empty meditation hall. He gave her a cushion to sit on, showed her how to hold her hands in a circle so her thumbs touched at the top with her other fingers in a bowl below, and told her only: "Think of the moon."

She closed her eyes. She breathed. She thought of the moon. After a while, one of her legs started to hurt. Badly. She had no idea how long she'd been sitting there and no idea how long she had left to sit. Her leg was driving her crazy. But she still had that competitive streak from her childhood, so she decided to tough it out. She sat, and she sat, and she sat.

After a while, she noticed something. The leg would hurt, then it would hurt more until it required all of her attention. Just when it seemed like there was no way she could sit any longer, the pain would start to fade, either from her awareness or from her body (she couldn't tell the difference anymore), until it was gone. She felt a sense of euphoria, just like she was the moon, and she'd come around from the shadow of the Earth into the light of the sun, shining fully on her.

Then, the leg would start to hurt again, and she would come around the other side of the Earth, back into the shadow.

This happened again and again and again and again until even the sense of time started to dissolve. Finally, the monk struck a metal bowl with a wooden hammer, ringing out three chimes, and the woman opened her eyes. The monk bowed to her, and she bowed back. She limped back up the wooden path to her room -- her leg was dead asleep by then -- and got out the journal she always kept with her.

This is what she wrote:

"Pain is temporary. Pleasure is temporary. The one who pays attention is eternal."

When she told me this story, she said that it was the emptiness inside her that allowed her to finally hear the voice of her spirit once she forced herself to sit in silence and let the pain and pleasure come and go, come and go.

For her entire childhood and well into her adulthood, my friend suffered because there wasn't enough love and attention to go around in her family. I've often wondered about the suffering caused by the illusion of "never enough." For Hitler, there could never be enough power over others. Never enough superiority, the death and destruction caused by this unquenchable desire for <u>more</u> can hardly be comprehended by our human brains.

Sometimes, though, suffering through scarcity -- or apparent scarcity -- can bring us around to the realization that, in each present moment, we all have exactly what we need. I recognize that the world is full of famine, war, and injustice. Can I honestly say that a malnourished child living in fear of violence halfway around the world from me has exactly what they need?

According to the rules of the world -- no, they don't.

But according to the rules of the spirit, anyone can awaken to inner joy and peace at any time. Sometimes, the feeling of being driven by "never enough" is the very thing that leads us to hear the voice of the spirit.

After my friend first awoke to the wholeness of her spirit in that monastery in Japan, she spent years seriously studying Zen meditation. Often, her leg would hurt, just the way it had in Japan. By simply paying quiet attention to it and not judging it as right or wrong, she found that the pain often disappeared -- and even when it didn't, it had no power over her. The same would happen with her emotions.

Even though she had long since forgiven her family, she would sometimes be overwhelmed by old feelings of rage and emptiness, just the way she used to feel as a child when her sister would run away, crash the car, or get drunk, and her parents would focus all their attention on her. She learned to acknowledge this feeling without attaching to it or pushing it away. After a lot of practice, she came to see that the pain just existed. It didn't belong to her -- or not to her spirit, anyway.

Every time a painful sensation or emotion arose, she learned to turn her attention to the inner voice of her spirit. "What is lacking in this moment?" she would ask.

And the answer would always return: "Nothing at all."

> When we listen to the voice of the ego, there is never enough of whatever we crave. When we learn to listen to the spirit, the present moment is all we need.

Chapter 10

Hearing Voices

Who the fuck are you? Really?

There are at least two voices in my head: the voice of my ego and the voice of my spirit. In reality, my ego speaks in countless different voices, changing its tune by the minute. It will say anything to try to get what it wants. When I listen to my ego, it's enough to drive me crazy with inner conflict. I truly am schizophrenic.

The voice of the spirit, on the other hand, never changes. It is eternal, and it is immortal. It only teaches one lesson: love.

The ego is motivated by the "scarcity principle." This is what makes us feel that we lack something to be happy. We search for it in people and possessions. It is only found within ourselves. It used to be true that every time I got something that I believed I wanted or needed, it made me happy for a bit. That is, until my ego convinced me that I needed something better, bigger, faster, more expensive, or just more.

The ego will lead you around in circles, forever chasing your tail. The most interesting thing about the ego is how effective it is at getting us to believe that it <u>is us</u>. We are taught to identify so strongly with our egos that we don't even realize there is another voice inside us -- watching quietly, speaking the truth, gently guiding and reminding us of our reason to be. This voice is the voice of our eternal spirit.

Anyone who knows me well will tell you that I have an enormous ego. It truly is tremendous. A work of art. When I was younger, following the voice of my ego led me to accomplish all kinds of things the world sees as valuable. I started and ran a successful business. I made gobs of money. I dated more beautiful women than I can count. None of it made me truly happy.

I got married young. My wife was a good-looking lady, and back then, she was fun to be around. We had a lot in common, or so it seemed on the surface. We both came from families with four boys and one girl. Both of us had tough parents -- although my wife's dad was a good person, which couldn't be said for my stepdad. Most importantly, we both liked to drink, fuck, and act like the immature idiots we were. We got married young for the wrong reasons, which seems to be a common mistake for people in our culture.

I was following my ego's script, which said I ought to do what everyone else did after they got married, so we had our first kid, a boy, followed pretty closely by a second, a girl. Ego said I was the breadwinner, so I went to work at a rental car company and my wife stayed home to take care of the kids.

One day, I was at work and I found myself bored out of my skull. Now I know that boredom is a surefire sign that I'm out of touch with the voice of my spirit, but back then, all I could hear was my ego telling me I had to do something -- anything -- to stop this awful feeling of emptiness and disconnection. The smart thing to do would be to turn inward to find the place where I felt whole and complete, but I was an idiot who'd never felt whole or complete a day in my life, so instead, I rolled a joint and went into the bathroom to smoke it.

Just my luck; my boss showed up while I was in there. I came out bleeding from the eyeballs and reeking of weed, and he fired me on the spot.

I went home, and when I told my wife I'd been fired, she slapped me across the face. I slapped her back. Oh, boy. That wasn't part of the script. I immediately got down on my knees and started begging for forgiveness. It didn't matter. I slept on the couch for a couple of nights. Eventually, we both kind of got over it, or at least we glossed over it and pretended to move on, but that was the beginning of the end. I got another job, and I never hit my wife again -- or any other woman -- but the fights got so bad being at home was like being in the seventh circle of hell. It took thirteen years for us to get a divorce.

After the divorce, I started thinking and learning about how to flip the script and figure out how I can be at peace and joy constantly. Ultimately, I realized that all my misery was created in an attempt to protect my ego. I had been fighting, justifying, rationalizing, and vindicating my self-created ego. The ego is the false narrative in my head of who I was, am, and who I thought I wanted to be in this life. The creation of my culture and education of the person I should be, not the real me.

My ego is the self I made in my mind, not my true self. This ego was made by my conditioning, culture, and experiences. My ego was a smart, funny, hardworking asshole who was always right and defended the roles I played while navigating this physical world. But now I understood that once I ended this life, all this fiction would end with me. My spirit and loving self would be the only thing that lived on. My only true self is my eternal spiritual self. My ego is complete bullshit because it can change with a whim, while my eternal self lives on forever in its natural state.

As I get older, my ego is constantly telling me to worry about not having enough money to support myself in the style to which I am accustomed until I die. But no one pays me to worry about money, so what's the point? Better to take action and make more money if that's my priority. I can ask for a raise, spend less, get another job, kidnap someone for ransom, create an email scam, or other entrepreneurial endeavors. But what will bring me peace and happiness? Money? It hasn't yet.

When I was married, one of the sources of tension between me and my wife (besides the fact that I was a huge asshole and she was a huge pain in the ass) was that she was a planner, and I liked to keep things spontaneous. When we went on a trip together, my wife would need to know where we were going to stop for gas, what and when we were going to eat, how we were going to keep the kids entertained, and exactly what time we were going to arrive at our destination.

I liked to put the car in drive and hit the accelerator.

Neither way is right or wrong by itself -- it's all about what gives you the most peace and contentment. Our egos are obsessed with planning and control because we have been taught that without planning, the future will be bad. Yet it is all the planning and attempts to control that cause us stress and keep us from being aware that something wonderful is already happening around us.

The ego creates stories in our minds that bring us fear. When there is fear in my mind, I start seeing danger everywhere. I used to live in fear because my ego would make me think that any confrontations would lead to an explosive situation with another person, and I wasn't down for that. I was assuming the worst without cause. I would end up avoiding confrontation and that too would make me unhappy. When I learned to confront others with love and without condition by saying things like, "I'm not your judge and don't care what you do, but your constant lateness is making me not want to hang out with you," I would feel better and get a less angry response.

The ego is that voice in your head telling you that change is bad and scary and that doing what you know will keep you safe.

"Don't be weak; stand up for yourself."

"Don't let people take advantage of you; fight for what is yours!"

The ego is always there like a good friend, telling you that you are right and should stay the course. Does anyone ever really think they are a bad person, regardless of all their bad behavior? I have asked mean people and chronic liars why they behave the way they do, and every single one of them defended their behavior indignantly as if I were the problem. Over time, I've learned that I can't change anyone but myself. Change is an eternal constant. But getting others to change the way we want them to isn't.

My ego judges on an ever-changing scale, fears death, and attacks when challenged. The craziest part of all this is that I have been so ingrained to believe my ego that it acts like an opaque curtain, blocking out the truth. The truth is in the spirit, not this world. The curtain blocks the simple and obvious to the point that sometimes I don't even remember the truth. Getting back to remembering the truth is the practice I speak about throughout this book. Whenever I'm stressed or fearful, I consciously bring myself back to the truths in this book and that centers me. Before I knew this, I would fret over something for days and weeks. Through practice, I spend no more than a minute or two now getting the craziness out of my head.

Instead of stressing about whether I will have "enough" of whatever I think I need, I can now calmly decide what it is I am lacking and evaluate if I truly need it to be happy. Whenever I get stressed out and anxious, I stop, center my mind by getting into the present moment, and ask myself, "What is it that I need at this moment?"

I've done this a thousand times and have always come up with the same answer. Nothing. That calms me.

When I allowed my ego to be in charge of my thinking, I was sleepwalking through life. Days and weeks have gone by when I haven't fed my spirit at all because that would require a change in my routine. My ego created an impossible situation. No matter what I achieved, I realized I was still never satisfied. My ego was constantly shifting from one goal to another: more stuff, better relationships, more money, better job, faster car.

Deep down, we all know we are not our ego and that our ego is a false construct that each of us has created for protection from dangers that mostly don't exist in the present moment. We fear past harms, and we fear an imaginary future. It's all part of our unique story. We love our stories and embrace and embellish them daily.

The world we know hasn't been imposed upon us from the outside. It has been presented to us and created by each of our own thought systems from within. The fear-based mind seeks love from the world. The love-based mind brings love to the world. The ego is so persistent that we believe it's real.

> **When we want something to be real, we can make it real.**

To defeat my ego thoughts, I had to recognize them and stop responding to them. Notice the anxiety and depression-inducing thoughts and determine that I would no longer entertain them. I had to take the emotion and fight out of my daily life. As I've learned to live more consciously, in the present now, I finally have a little bit of sanity in my life. I've stopped trying to negotiate with my ego to bring an end to the feelings of fear, dissatisfaction, boredom, and loneliness. I now make it a daily goal to eliminate my ego and only live with acceptance of what is, unconditional equality for others, and learning what the universe is trying to teach me.

Would you prefer to be a hostage to the ego or a host to peace?

Although we create and defend our egos, they are not who we truly are.

Chapter 11

Courtroom Drama

Think of all your daily judgments. Now consider if any of them are true.

When I moved out of the house I used to share with my ex-wife, I eventually found a place in a nice part of town that I could barely afford. It was a brick colonial with a big backyard, complete with an apple tree. Inside, there was a kitchen, dining room, and living room with a real fireplace, and upstairs were two bedrooms -- one for me, one for the kids -- and an office.

By this point in my life, I'd started a successful company modifying and selling vans for people in wheelchairs. I should have been able to afford a nice house and a nice car and a nice vacation every year, but the divorce had been contentious, and I was paying alimony in addition to child support, so I drove a beater, and the vacations would have to wait.

If I thought living with my ex-wife was the worst kind of hell, going through the divorce was a close second. We both hired lawyers and lobbed judgments and accusations back and forth like grenades. I drank too much, worked too hard, and was never around. (Valid.) She was controlling, an emotional wreck, and she virtually never spoke to me except to criticize me. (Also, valid.)

When the divorce was finalized, I thought I'd be able to put all this courtroom drama to bed. But something else happened instead. I got a dog to keep me company, a sheepdog I named Stahoo after my grandfather. The one thing Stahoo loved most was chasing a tennis ball I'd spend hours throwing for him in my big backyard. The other thing he loved was jumping over the fence when I went inside. It was a six-foot fence, and he'd jump right over it, cut through my neighbor's yard, and go sit on my front stoop until I noticed he was gone and went to let him in. He never went anywhere else -- never ran away, or chased a cat down the street, or got into any trouble at all. He was a good dog, one of the best.

The problem was my neighbor, the one whose yard Stahoo landed in when he jumped over the fence. John was an older guy, married with a couple of grown sons, and his wife seemed nice enough, but he hated dogs.

Dogs!

What kind of maniac hates dogs?

One day I got home from work to find an envelope with my name on it taped to my front door. There was a note inside. It said:

"If I see your dog in my yard again, I will call the dog pound. -- Your neighbor, John"

That was the beginning of a new kind of courtroom drama. Only this one took place in my head. I took the note and tossed it into the fireplace. I never said a word about it to John, and Stahoo kept on jumping over my fence into his yard, and he never called anyone about it as far as I knew. But I became a little obsessed.

I'd tell anyone who came over to my house, "That's John who lives over there, he's a real asshole."

I developed a list of judgments against John a mile long, almost none of them having to do with Stahoo.

He should cut his hair shorter, the balding fuck.

Those dandelions he let grow on his lawn in the summer were a disgrace.

He drove his car in winter without warming up the engine first, the idiot.

I even started in on the wife and kids.

She looked nice, but she probably tortured kittens for fun.

They had a basketball hoop in the driveway, and when the two sons came home for the holidays, they'd play out there -- and, boy, did they stink it up. My grandmother could sink more free throws than them.

He should do this. She should do that. They're all too this, that, and the other thing.

I'm ashamed to admit this, but the courtroom drama in my mind went on until John sold the house and a nice couple my age moved in with a labrador retriever.

Now, I just have to laugh at myself. Why would I spend so much mental energy judging other people? (Even if John was an a-hole.) When I think of that note today, all I can think is how funny it is that he threatened to call the "dog pound." What was this, Lady and the Tramp?

It would have been nice if the problem was John and not me. But it took me many years to learn the lesson I should have taken away from my imaginary courtroom drama. The lesson was that my judgments kept me in a state of negativity and for all I know, they were completely wrong. Even if they were right, all those judgments did was keep me in a state of mental conflict. Besides, all of my mental judging and jurying had zero effect on anyone else except me, and it wasn't positive.

When my brain was young, nimble, and stupid, the damned thing constantly judged everyone and everything. I couldn't get that inner voice to stop ranking and rating things and others as good or bad. Poor John was in good company. <u>That person swears too much, he's too fat or too skinny, her teeth are crooked, their hair looks dirty, they talk too much, they don't say anything, they speak nonsense,</u> and on and on, forever.

Of course, I judged myself as well -- although not as harshly, because I judge myself from my intentions and not my behavior. Eventually, I realized that I was doing that with everyone. Judging only their behavior and not their intentions.

Today, I know that I am constantly and incessantly being judged by others, especially because I live a non-standard life. Allowing other people's judgments to be my mirror used to cause me nothing but insecurity. Even if one person thinks I'm great today, someone else will think I'm a crackpot the next. It's a rollercoaster ride and not the fun kind.

For years, I tried hard to get other people to judge me more positively. I might as well have had "LIKE ME" tattooed across my forehead. Over time, I have learned that all my judgments and the judgments of others toward me mean nothing.

I first started to understand that my judgments were suspect, thanks to my younger brother's wife. When they first got together, man, I couldn't stand that woman! She was too fussy, too uptight, too judgmental. (Oh, the irony!)

But slowly, over time, especially after she gave birth to my twin niece and nephew, other kinds of judgments started creeping in.

She was a supportive partner to my brother. She was a hard worker and pulled her weight. She was a kind and loving, yet fierce and protective mother -- the kind of mother I used to wish I had. I even noticed that she had one of the most radiant smiles I'd ever seen, and I came to appreciate her cooking, too.

I could just say, "Well, I got proven wrong," or "She grew on me," but instead I got curious. Why had I judged her so harshly to begin with? Could it be that I was a little jealous of my brother's attention and affection? We'd always been the closest of my siblings. Then I remembered I never liked any of my brother's girlfriends. Huh. Did my brother have lousy taste in women, or was something off with my judgments?

Once I began to understand that my judgments were suspect, I set about re-evaluating the ever-changing, elastic measuring stick I was using to judge. Every single person has their own individual ideas about what's right, what's wrong, and what the other fellow should be doing with his life. I am the only person in the world who has my exact set of rules for adjudication. This alone convinced me that, as fallible, ego-driven humans, our judgments of ourselves and others are meaningless.

What a liberating concept!

When I took a closer look, I found that my judgments were almost always incorrect, insignificant, and futile. I could judge another person as an asshole, but that didn't make them one. More times than not, I judged a person as someone I didn't like, but once I got to know them, I learned I was wrong. It was just the negativity and competitiveness I had created in my mind. Its only useful purpose was to keep me stuck in insecurity and unhappiness.

From the moment we are born, we are graded, evaluated, charted, ranked, labeled, measured, weighed, compared, and judged in an attempt to bring some order to a chaotic world. How true is any of this? I smile inside when someone tells me that they were labeled a "genius" in elementary school. Why have they never been successful in this world? Maybe because they keep expecting the rest of the world to see their genius and give them what they think they deserve. The real "genius" would learn that any label is fiction.

When we are judged, it becomes our mission to either confirm or shed those labels put on us by others. Even if we respect the other people who judge us, who are they to define who we are? That's no one's job but our own.

When you judge others -- good, bad, better, or worse -- ask yourself by what scale are you judging or being judged? Whose scale? Who's the judge? What are the exact measurements? I know that I judge others to boost my self-concept, but in reality, my judgments have exactly the opposite effect. When I think that I don't like someone, often it's because they are behaving like I used to do -- and now I think I know better. I see parts of me that I don't like, so I judge others harshly to build myself up. But inside, I know the truth. Now, I see nothing but myself when I look at them.

> I have come to realize that when I judge another person harshly, I am not defining them but myself.

Judging others is how I rationalize my bad behavior. My ego is constantly convincing me that I'm right -- but right about what? Judging others as not as righteous, decent, fit, nice, considerate, fair, smart, generous, or generally worthy as it used to make me feel good for a fleeting minute until I realized it was me I was defining.

Not only was I beginning to realize that my judgments were mostly pointless, but they were also the cause of my internal strife. My constant judging was a huge barrier to my inner peace.

Our judgments are created by our unique past experiences and learning -- not objective truth. But I don't want to see the world for what it isn't; I am seeking truth and reality. I no longer care about whom I think is a jerk. By not judging others, I immediately stopped giving a crap about others' judgments about me. (Unless they were glowing.) When I stopped judging everyone, I stopped judging myself. I started playing this mental game when I was around others. I would be the scientific observer with no emotion other than joy and no judgment. That was complete and final liberation.

I also realized that often my judgments were creating situations where I would anticipate the outcome of a situation. My expectations gave the situation a negative power over me. My boss called and I expected to get scolded, or one of my kids called and I would assume they wanted something from me. These thoughts would make me anxious and annoyed, and often I was wrong. I started wondering: How much of my life had I wasted assuming bad shit would happen when it rarely did? Even when it did, my prior anxiety did nothing to improve the situation or help create a better response or outcome.

As part of my judging ego, I would create imaginary "roles" for people and then get mad when they didn't behave in the way I thought they should. Roles have changed over time, so how "true" can they be? Every role I accept for myself limits me in growth because it creates an imaginary border on my thinking that I take on as defining me. This goes on until I stop and awaken to the unreality of these fictional roles. The more I become attached to these roles and masks, the less I can openly embrace those who are different than me.

As I grow to be a better and happier soul, I am learning to observe situations without judgment, condition, or emotion, and I am seeing a whole other beautiful world that was previously blocked out. It's okay to believe that you are on the right path as long as you know that yours isn't the only path. By accepting what is without judgment, I remain free and at peace. My pursuit of oneness and connection with all other people, rather than my own individuality, has brought me joy. The pursuit of uniqueness and difference through judgment has only brought pain.

Our judgments are responsible for all the murder, hate, racism, chaos, and turmoil in the world -- and they aren't even true. Maybe I think my judgments are true, but the person I judge doesn't. One of my favorite hobbies used to be sitting around with like-minded people and those who would listen, shitting all over someone else. They're a loser, a bad parent, lazy, or any other negative judgments designed to build myself up at the expense of another. Since I stopped doing that and started knowing that I don't fully understand anyone's motives or intentions besides my own, I am much happier and the universe has stopped sending me as much conflict as before. Giving up judgments and conditionality has silenced my ego's voice. I've accepted that true wisdom isn't judgment but the relinquishment of it. I recognize that now I am seeing the world as it really is.

> Because our judgments of others are temporary and biased, they are not true. When I stopped judging others, it was me who was set free.

Chapter 12

The Lies That Bind

Are all of your relationships equal and unconditional?

When I began to study peace, I found that almost all my internal conflicts involved relationships. It began when I expected others to behave in a way that was acceptable to me. Was I getting as much from the other person as I was giving? Did they overtly show me the respect that I felt I deserved? Did they have something I wanted? Could I manipulate or control them for my own satisfaction? Were they doing that to me?

Growing up, I learned that interactions with other people depended on who they were according to the tribal rules of the nuclear family. I was required to love my family -- even the mean, nasty members of my family -- but be wary of anyone else. No fighting allowed! (Except at home with the family I was supposed to love. And because there were four boys, we could beat the shit out of each other. Anywhere outside the family, it would get us an assault charge.)

And, because my relationship with my parents was anything but unconditional, I learned that I had to hustle to be loved. Only I could never hustle hard enough. I spent a lot of my young years in conflict with my parents because I couldn't -- or wouldn't -- be who they wanted me to be. I never did earn their approval, but I did learn to stop caring about it. What a relief!

Still, as a young man, I thought the "right" relationship would cure me of my chronic feelings of lack and dissatisfaction. Maybe if I found a woman who loved me the way my mother never did, I would feel at peace. Believe me, I tried this out on a lot of women before I woke up. That wake-up call came sometime during the years leading up to my divorce. If I could love someone and be loved, and that made me happy -- but it was only temporary and conditional -- what good was that to my immortal spirit?

I still search for happiness in relationships with other people. And I find it, quite often, in people who inspire me, make me laugh, make me think, or even just help me have a good time. But I no longer give away my inherent power to be happy. I try to interact with everyone unconditionally because I have found that it's the only way I can ensure interactions that increase my happiness. They can be fully who they are and I can be fully who I am without playing mind games.

If you consider it objectively, relationships create the most conflict in our lives. If you want to find happiness in life, you have to figure out how to manage relationships. You start by managing yourself.

Even though there are a lot of different types of relationships, I like to break them down into two types: Those I can leave easily and those I can't. Family, fellow employees, neighbors -- those bonds are tougher to break. Everyone else is in my life of my choosing and can be removed or blocked on any whim.

I have found that it's not the people I leave who cause me lasting pain but the people I don't leave, even when my spirit is screaming at me to cut ties. The selfish friend, the one who constantly feels like a victim, the broke "friend" who won't keep a job but will always take a handout, the person who is never happy and has a negative judgment for everyone. You get the picture. I have learned to move on from relationships when it makes me happier to do so. I used to try and "fix" people, but all I did was ensure that I stayed broken.

Then there are the relationships that are toxic but harder to get out of: your partner, your coworkers, your family. Although many of us convince ourselves that these relationships are required, I discovered that some truly weren't. These are the relationships that have hurt me the most and caused me an inordinate amount of resentment, discontent, and internal dissonance. This happened because I couldn't accept that the relationships offered nothing but conflict. My ego had taught me to compete and win all the battles, so when I met with conflict in my relationships, I behaved as I was taught. I argued, debated, reasoned, used logical arguments, quoted scientific studies, used inductive and deductive lingo, and still, I never seemed to get anyone to think differently. I had learned from my stepfather that digging my feet in felt better than submitting to someone else's wrong thinking.

I didn't know there was another option.

Then I realized that if you say "Republican" and I say "Democrat," it's a tie. Stalemate. No blood. Whether I get mad or I stay happy, it's still a tie. Besides, I won't give a shit in an hour -- so why give a shit for a second?

Most importantly, though, I realized that simply letting go of conflict and the need to be "right" wasn't submission. It wasn't the same as the abuse I'd suffered as a child. Instead, letting go removed a long-standing barrier to my inner peace and happiness. I had been trying to "save" many people by sticking to my guns and promoting my views. <u>Get rid of that friend, get a better job, tell them what you really think, blah, blah, blah.</u>

None of it fixed anything.

I wish I had learned this when I was younger, but when I stopped trying to change others and accepted their behavior without conditions, it had an unexpected side effect. More people began to stop and listen to me. I would start a tough conversation with, "I don't give a shit what you do because I'm not your judge..." and then I could say almost anything I wanted. That's because I was saying it without challenging anyone. I spoke with no malice or negativity, and the other person sincerely felt that from me. It transformed arguments into discussions. If someone disagreed with me, and I felt they couldn't teach me anything, the conversation was over! I couldn't control their behavior, and we both knew it. I was giving them the unconditional ability to exert their free will, and I could comment on it, but it wasn't mine to control.

As I got better at approaching relationships with no attachments and no conditions, I became much happier. I began to understand that the best relationships are between absolute equals, with no master and servant. Tied -- nothing to nothing. It hit me that the same behavior that had been causing me angst wasn't going to suddenly give me peace. I had been getting annoyed at the same shit for 40 years! I would think that someone acted like an asshole or said something I didn't like, and I would immediately get irritated, disappointed, insecure, or even enraged. I could always feel myself getting mad and doing a slow boil, and every once in a while, I would actually let my cranium blow. I thought it felt good -- but afterward, I was disappointed in myself for losing control. I was just convincing myself that I was right. I wasn't.

When I was 17 years old, I fell in love with a girl named Katrina Summer. My first love and it was a doozy. The first cut is the deepest. The problem was Katrina was gorgeous, and I was immature, so I acted like a jealous, controlling asshole. I wanted to know what she was doing whenever we weren't together -- as if that made a difference to my happiness! If I saw her talking to another guy, I gave her the third degree. We only lasted a year, and then she broke up with me. Not only that, but she also didn't want anything to do with me. If she saw me coming down the hall, she turned the other way. That was a huge wake-up call. But it still took me years to stop trying to make the people in my life more like what I wanted them to be.

I know now that I can't isolate or control another person and remain at peace. I've tried for more than thirty years and still haven't been successful. I get frustrated and the others feel constrained. A relationship can't be healthy and enduring if one person wants to change the other against their will.

We are taught that the form of our relationships matters more than their content. Certain behaviors are expected and even required for relationships to endure. Monogamy, servitude, subordination, mutual dependence, and other controls have been put in place culturally to set the rules of "good" relationships. Yet, if we live by these rules, aren't we searching for love in bondage and control? The only way this works (and it only works temporarily) is when the other person allows and accepts the control. However, this can be revoked at any time, with or without cause.

For me to create a truly loving relationship, it must be unconditional. And since I cannot control another person, it is me who has to start. So, I begin every relationship with two rules. Rule one: no ownership. Unconditional equality. Rule two: no drama, just discussion and learning. Having these rules allows me to only concentrate on the content of the relationship, not the form. The best "me" shows up every time. If I act like a douchebag, you wouldn't want to see me again. If I don't, maybe you will. Simple.

Think about it. Most people you have met in your life are no longer in your life. That shows that meeting someone new is often the first step in parting ways. So, what is the purpose of these interactions and relationships? I believe it is to learn lessons, exchange knowledge (and maybe bodily fluids), learn love and kindness and move on.

Recently, one of my friends met someone and there was an immediate attraction between the two. They made out and went their separate ways. The next day, my friend was bombarded with texts and calls from this person, telling her he wanted a relationship with her and that she was not to see other people. My friend immediately blocked this person from her life. What an obvious and bold lesson, learned quickly. In the past, she would have spent too much time trying to get this person to see things her way, but to what end? If the other person thought they needed to change to maintain a relationship, they would have shown signs of that desire instead of trying to control my friend. In any case, I have learned that attempting to cure other people's insecurities is a fool's errand.

Now when I look at my relationships, I first decide the outcome I desire from this relationship. Not what I can get out of it, but what outcome? It's always love! No ownership and no drama. I do everything in my power to create that outcome. When it's not happening, I simply move on. Lesson learned -- no need for a harsher lesson.

Every action and thought we have is either loving or a call for love. The more I extend the loving me, the more I love others and they love me. This eliminates relationship conflict and keeps me at peace.

Everyone is connected through our humanity, so our differences are temporary and irrelevant.

We can only change ourselves.

> The only truly loving relationship is unconditional and among equals. Everything else is bondage. And not the fun, consensual kind.

Chapter 13

I Pray We Don't Get Fooled Again

Why do we teach lies and expect them to endure?

Teaching that dominance and oppression over others is the road to success is bullshit, and we all know it deep inside. It's a problem in our "little" relationships, the one-on-one relationships with family, lovers, neighbors, and so on. It's an even bigger problem when groups of people try to control and oppress other groups of people for their own gain.

I don't know if we can change the world's curriculum that is taught to our children, but we seriously should consider it. I'm not advocating for a total overhaul because I don't exactly know what is in all the course curriculums currently. What I do know is that we are graduating more unhappy, depressed, alienated, and cynical children than ever before. Not only is there a large degree of hypocrisy in the lessons, but we aren't looking to teach our children how not to keep going down the road of war, poverty, conflict, separation, and planetary destruction. In fact, we keep creating great warriors and corporate employees.

I think we should begin teaching them about our connectivity with all other living things and the fact that we are eternal souls here to learn love. Most people will think that you can't teach those things because it would combine the church and state teachings. I disagree because the main ideas I have written about in this book have not come from religious teachings but from new scientific evidence. Do the people who create the curriculums in our schools read and study these lines of thought? I doubt it but even if a few people do, they will be almost certainly dismissed by those who don't. Why not courses on conflict resolution, tolerance for diversity, the futility of negative judgments, and other topics talked about in this book? Is the truth so frightening that we can't bear to expose it to the light? I don't think having courses in these topics will turn out even more emotionally and spiritually damaged children, and I do believe it will do the opposite.

The rules of our culture teach that individuality is the goal. The rules of the spirit teach that we are all one. Are we stronger and better alone or with a shared purpose and mission? A grain of sand can do little on its own, but a beach works in harmony to hold back the ocean.

Having individuality drilled into our heads causes us to believe that we are one among many rather than connected to every living thing. I have prayed to God for more money, more safety and security, status, and revenge, all the while hoping that God will serve me with the unreal pleasures of the physical, ego-driven world. Hell, I had a God of sports betting, bigger houses, better cars, and so much more, but it wasn't until I stopped begging and started accepting that I found the real God of peace.

As I set out on my formal quest for the real reason we are living this life, I had to identify and understand what I had been conditioned to think by my education, culture, religion, and imposed biases because, in almost all cases, they were lies. Bullshit, horseshit, dogshit, baby shit, batshit, catshit, shit sandwich, pigshit, crock of shit, scared shit, shit yourself, take a shit and give a shit. We're all full of it, especially when proclaiming the "truth."

I have learned that by undoing my individuality and ego, the application of that knowledge creates a cumulative effect on my evolutionary and spiritual growth. I'm like a snowball rolling down a hill of wet, sticky snow, and my soul gets bigger and stronger with every turn. As I apply the knowledge of oneness and peace to my experiences, I no longer have to learn the same harsh lessons over and over.

I was brought up to be very competitive, to the point where not winning wasn't possible. Whether a game, an argument, a discussion, a car, or just about anything -- in my mind, I simply could not lose. I hated losing much more than I loved winning. Like the green flies that refuse to leave the shit pile, I kept returning to that buffet until I decided I could no longer delude myself. Now, at my much more ripened age, winning and losing are the same -- irrelevant. I find the fun in learning and being.

When I was starting as a bartender in a dive bar in central Pennsylvania, one of the town drunks was a guy named Fritz. One day, he was sitting at the bar, slapping himself in the face over and over. I said to him, "Fritz, why are you doing that?" He replied calmly, "Because it feels great when I stop." That summed up most of my chronically adversarial behavior, but it took me many years to learn the lesson of how good it felt when I stopped.

The only true things are those that are eternal and live on past our current lives and limited egos. Our spirits, the energy and spirits of other living beings, and the vast universe we don't understand -- these are eternal. Nothing else. When I first became aware of this truth, it was unsettling and even a little scary. Everything I had learned from this world was no longer as important to me. If we know we can't flap our arms and fly, would we waste our whole lives trying?

My whole life I had been faced with the choice between grievance and conflict or peace and love. Now, I would formally begin choosing the latter. No more would I allow a fear-based worldly thought system to make me keep flapping my arms to rise above it. I would rise above it merely by changing my mind.

This world teaches many ways of thinking that are the opposite of the truth. "If I only had <u>more</u>, I would be happier."

This thinking has caused me a lot of unhappiness because it seemed like I was lacking something. On the other hand, if I accepted what I had, having less would make me happy.

Trying to control another person gives you less control over them. Trying hard to avoid pain and struggles is a pain and a struggle in and of itself. Detailed planning may make you think you have everything under control -- but when the plans change, frustration and stress become the plan. My competitiveness brought me temporary ego boosts and burned me up with discontent. Neither satisfied.

I learned that my mind had created false truths in virtually every part of my life, and my happiness suffered because of it. Yet these beliefs were as real to me as the nose on my face. Through my categorizing, arbitrating, adjudicating, umping, decreeing, swearing, gullibility, and wishful thinking, I had invented my own set of "truths." My mental narrative had rarely ever shut the fuck up. It still hasn't. But now I know how to recognize it and stop listening by redirecting my ego's voice to my eternal spirit's voice.

I started wondering: If there is only the truth of eternity, and I had become conscious of this truth, what now? I was excited to spend more of my life reflecting on truth rather than the events of the physical world! Now, I no longer get emotionally attached because I set an outcome to maintain my inner peace, knowing that this interaction will be forgotten by tomorrow, next week, next year, or next century.

We are taught that when someone hurts you, a response to get even is required. But does it take more strength to fight back or to simply accept the lesson delivered quietly? I contend that it's the latter, but it's not what this world teaches and gives medals for.

None of it will matter soon. I have learned to love what is because the only other option is to not love.

What we believe of the real truth is irrelevant.

The truth is.

Chapter 14

Practice Makes Perfect

The options we have in any given situation are usually few and obvious.

Often, I feel like I am a therapist without the degree since many of my friends want to talk to me about issues in their lives. They start by saying, "I want to know what you would do in this situation..." and then proceed to get into it. Although my advice has a deep foundation in what you have just read, the nuances of the responses are designed to fit the specific situations as well as the person asking for the advice.

When it comes to relationship advice, there are never many great options at first. You either have to decide to stay in the relationship and forgive the other person of any transgressions you feel they have made, or you have to start thinking about leaving the relationship behind. When I knew my marriage was over because the fighting was getting worse, not better, it still took me years to get up the nerve to formally end it.

I see that in many relationships now, one or more of the participants aren't truly happy. I believe that relationship happiness is more of a continuum than an on-off button. Many times, when people come to me to ask my opinion, it's about their romantic relationship.

Recently, a long-time friend came over and was crying because she had just caught her husband cheating on her. Obviously distraught, she proceeded to tell me the details of how she came home early from work one day and there was her husband having sex in the living room with this other woman.

They had been married for more than 30 years and had three grown children who had long since moved out of the house.

I asked her if she wanted to leave her husband, and she told me, "No." I asked if her husband wanted to leave her. Again, "No." "Well, if you two want to stay together, it's only going to work if you can forgive him and trust him again. If you are constantly reminding him of his dalliances and laying guilt trips on him, it will never work out. If you hold anything against him, your relationship will be one of conflict and pain. If that happens, you two may still stay in the same house, but you will be miles away emotionally. You must do the work on yourself to let this go and be happy in the relationship once again. Can you do this?" She quietly replied, "I'm not sure."

I told her, "Even if you find out later that you can't let this go, you are always free to leave. Put the work into the relationship to see if you want to stay and, equally importantly, does he want to stay? His behavior going forward will tell you that."

At this point, I don't know how they're doing, but I do know that my message was difficult for her to hear. She wasn't ready to forgive him at that point in time, but she knew I was right in my assessment. There is no need for anger or revenge, but there is a need for clear thinking and more love, no matter how their relationship turns out. Determine the outcome you want and put all of your best energy into that, all the while understanding that you can't control anyone but yourself.

Often, friends approach me asking about soulmates and romantic relationships. Although I do believe there are soulmates for some of us, I don't think focusing a lot of attention on looking for the perfect soulmate partner is healthy or emotionally profitable. The people I know who are consumed with looking for their soulmate are in some ways broken because they think there is someone out there that, if they just meet, will fix and complete them. What they haven't learned yet is that until they fix themselves, all they are doing is dragging another partner into their drama. If they find someone who they think is their soulmate, now you have a broken self and a broken soulmate. Maybe that works, but I'm betting the under. The insecure and unevolved person repels the secure and evolving person away from them.

Another common complaint I get from friends is their dissatisfaction with their job. I first delve into whether the problem is actually with the work or is it with the people one has to work with. If the actual work is the problem, then we go down the path of, "If you could spend 40 hours a week doing anything, what would you want that to be?" I've known people with miserable jobs who like the work and people with fun jobs who are miserable. What I have found in most cases is that the difference between loving your work or hating it is the decisions you make in your head. Either way, if you don't like what you do, change it. You have all the power.

If the people you work with are the problem, start working on changing that too -- in your mind. If you choose to stay in that job, stop giving those people the inordinate power to take away your happiness. After all, they can't take your power of joy unless you consciously give it to them. I'm not saying it's going to be easy to change your thought process, but I am saying it's worth it to start working on your happiness right away.

It seems as though parents and family members are a source of unhappiness for many people, as it was for me for years. We must learn that our parents learned how to parent from parents who knew nothing except how they were raised, and they came out just fine. Unhappy and little.

By blaming your parents for your depression or anxiety, you are saying that you know what they did is wrong, so it's not your fault. It's your parents' fault for being shitty parents and not protecting you. I also know people who were brought up with good families and good parents, and they, too, have a long list of grievances caused by their good families. But when does that end? What options do you have? I think there are only two options -- take accountability for your own life or blame someone else.

Keep the good shit they gave you and shed the negative shit in your life and only then will you break the cycle of unhappiness and insecurity. When you keep the negative aspects of your upbringing in the now, you are saying that there was value in the way you were treated. Only you can decide if the way you were raised made you better or broke your spirit, and regardless of the one you choose, now is the time to stop being a victim to it. Hopefully, your bad parents taught you how not to parent.

The potentially more dangerous parents are those who love their children unconditionally and teach them to swallow their wrong beliefs about the world because children who have a completely loving childhood will swallow poop if their parents teach it. There are religious sects that create generations of thoughtless followers because they know that loving their children and making them part of the group will stop critical thinking in many of those kids. This will ensure the longevity and success of the congregation.

In large part, my advice always centers on not engaging in drama and misery -- yours or mine -- because if I do, I make it real. None of it is real because it's all temporary and most will be forgotten soon. Often, when someone is telling me a story about their own drama, I turn it around and ask, "What do you think the lesson for you is in this situation?" I have found this changes the conversation from one of victimization to that of empowerment.

There is only one thing in the whole universe that can keep us from being happy -- our decisions toward happiness. One of the greatest decisions to alleviate stress is not to be attached to any specific outcomes. Just allow the world to gently unfold with you in it spreading love.

> Intelligent advice on having better relationships is often simple if we choose to hear it.

Chapter 15

War Pigs

Making War Just for Fun

The elephant in the room when we talk about peace and the connection of all humans is our love of war. It's so profitable for the few. When I googled "How many wars are currently going on in the world?" according to war-memorial.net, there are 30! And the United States, aka the world's peacekeeper, has a hand in many. Currently, the United States has more than 750 military bases in over 80 different countries around the world at a cost of around $180 billion annually. Even when we aren't actually shooting the rockets at others, we certainly are selling high-tech weapons to whoever will pay for them. We don't seem to care about the total death and destruction these weapons of mass destruction cause because we make so much money selling them. And our government has found it beneficial to keep spreading fear about our enemies and threats, all the while glorifying the war effort. I don't know about you, but I wouldn't feel less safe if we closed down half of those bases and used the $90 billion to help improve our local society. Most of the time, we get sucked into wars because the locals are shooting or attacking our bases because they don't want us there anyway.

But how do we protect our interests throughout the world? What other countries have global interests? They all do, but only the United States is rich enough to occupy the world with guns, bombs, and money.

The other day, I decided to start counting the number of times I would see some message or advertisement promoting the United States military. Literally, by noon, I stopped counting at 21. Banners, billboards, commercials, ads, bumper stickers, signs, plaques, memorials, and more all reminded me to support our heroes, be a patriot, take off my ball cap, put my hand on my heart, and sing out loud for the United States of America!

As a country, the United States accounts for almost 40% of all military expenditures worldwide. In 2022, we spent $877 billion on the military, which is more than the next 11 countries combined. China spends one-third of the US, while Russia spends one-tenth.

I don't believe that this spending is really a case of our country wanting world peace but more a case of promoting capitalism. As a society, we would rather blow up the world and destroy it than question or control capitalism. We have been conditioned from the earliest years that socialism or communism is worth fighting against despite the problems that capitalism has created. But when I think about the whole of life on this planet, can it really be defined by 3 or 4 words that completely define everything? I'm not saying that capitalism is better or worse than the other societal constructs. But I am saying that if we want to stop wealth inequality, the inhumane treatment of workers for profit, our military-industrial complex, and the destruction of the planet for net earnings, we should start standing up against this. No one can convince me that we can't solve these problems except with continued complicity in the current groupthink.

One of the things that confuses me is why women feed into the male aggression. Should a mother send their child over to a foreign country to die in battle for a religious disagreement?

How is it that the religious right is supporting a presidential candidate who wants to build a wall to keep poor and needy souls out of a country that is so rich and we could give them a better life? Jesus never built a wall or even talked about turning our backs on those in need. If it were up to a lot of people in this country, they would have us electrify the wall with enough current to cause people who touch it to catch on fire. Then we could all toast weenies on their burning bodies and have a belly laugh, especially as the little children from the migrants burn.

So, how do we fix this without trying to control others? I just know that I can only believe in my views, share them when I can, and live in peace so others can see my complete contentment. Maybe in this life I can't influence others in power to rethink their war pig mentality, but maybe I can influence one other person. Then maybe they can influence one other person and the cycle of peace slowly builds momentum. I feel that I can stop the war mentality because if I don't believe it, I have only one other choice and that's to become part of it.

I've heard others argue that our second amendment to the Constitution guarantees that we can own guns, and apparently, as large of guns as someone will build. This belief has contributed to almost two mass shootings a day in this country -- every day of the year! What I calmly say is that when the Constitution was written, we believed we needed guns because we were still killing the British, the Indians, and our disobedient slaves. Has the world changed since 1776? Have we gotten any smarter or more rational?

Trying to stop the war pigs is better than never trying and it can't be done with force. I want the point of my life to be love and love doesn't build walls or teach separation from other living beings. Love just is. All-encompassing. Blissful. Complete. Final.

> We don't need more guns and war.
> We need more love. War stops with me.

Chapter 16

The (There Is No) End

Don't you want to know what the point of your life is?

So, if we are eternal, most of our beliefs are wrong, and our only tasks are to gain knowledge and spread love -- what should we <u>do</u> with these temporary human lives of ours?

I don't have all the answers. But I do know that the times in my life that I have felt the most human and at peace were those times when I unconditionally gave to another soul in need. Volunteering at a shelter, soothing a crying child or anxious pet, giving a few bucks to a homeless person, or any act of selfless kindness has always been the way I feel the most at peace. I wonder why I don't do it more often.

If we live on and this life is one of spiritual growth, one of many lives, then there must be a Source that has created all of this beauty and love. This Source has given every soul free will and the opportunity to gain the universal knowledge of love. There is no greater state of being.

We are taught to pray for the things we want, but this line of thinking supposes that the Source that we pray to is our servant, waiting to be ordered for Its next task. For this final chapter, let's call the Source "God" and leave any negative or uncomfortable connotations out of the mix, at least in this reading. (There is no gender intended when I use the word "God" because there is no differentiation between living souls in the universe.)

It is said that God created us in their image. I also believe that we returned the favor by creating God in our image. Vengeful, jealous, judgmental, and insecure -- but don't worry, our creation isn't true. Because God is eternal and none of our worldly beliefs are.

Only our souls and love are eternal because hate and conflict are not our natural state. So, if God is eternal love, there is no duality in the universe except what our egos have created and fostered. Wait -- no good versus evil where something can rise up and defeat God?! We are the problem?

All the signs point to "yes," but we hate being wrong.

God wants us to learn love and happiness as our birthright. As I go through this life, one of the main roles I consistently play is that of the scientific observer, remaining calm and objective at all times, learning from the lesson that is unfolding in front of me at any given moment. In this world, we all have to be on guard, calculating who has the power to help us, give us what we want, or keep us from getting it. In eternity, it's simple. We all have all the power.

I now know to put as much effort into my spiritual growth as I put into adorning my physical body. I have learned that most of my misery in the past was believing that I had no power to control my situation. I may not have the power to do certain things, but I have all the power to not feel bad about them. I know that I can't have what I don't choose, so I have started choosing exactly what I want to achieve.

I learned that living with conflict is perpetual and choosing to stop all conflict is final and complete. No longer am I a victim to my past because I have chosen to see it differently -- as lessons, not self-definitions. I have stopped judging others harshly or with pettiness and live unconditionally among all people. I can't control them and they can't control me. I now understand that the rules of this material world are not the same rules my spirit seeks to learn. I can follow the rules of this world as it suits me or ignore them if they don't. By following the rules of the spirit, however, I am graced with love, contentment, and peace. Why would anyone ignore these?

Now, before going into any situation, I ask God to guide me in being their messenger. That always fills me with warm comfort and makes the situation magical for all who wish to experience it that way.

Since change is the only constant, we must understand that the universe is one of constant change and growth. Some will fear this and cling to the good old days, while I will excitedly embrace the next moment when I can learn anew.

Whenever I get to a place where I am stressed, anxious, angry, or fearful, I know that there are two choices to pursue.

The first is to remain on the path of chaos, hypocrisy, and conflict.

The other is to choose forgiveness, surrender, and freedom. There are no other options to select.

Would you rather be a host to love or a hostage to your ego? We will be led back to love by our will, not by force.

When we give anything away, love or hate, it is increased because it is immediately doubled. Everything we extend is immediately increased. I want only to put love into the universe to increase it.

I hope you will join me.

Made in the USA
Las Vegas, NV
23 June 2024

91368581R00066